T0260879

Data Mining and Machine Learning in Building Energy Analysis

Series Editor
Serge Petiton

Data Mining and Machine Learning in Building Energy Analysis

Frédéric Magoulès
Hai-Xiang Zhao

WILEY

First published 2016 in Great Britain and the United States by ISTE Ltd and John Wiley & Sons, Inc.

ISTE Ltd
27-37 St George's Road
London SW19 4EU
UK

www.iste.co.uk

John Wiley & Sons, Inc.
111 River Street
Hoboken, NJ 07030
USA

www.wiley.com

Library of Congress Control Number: 2015958612

British Library Cataloguing-in-Publication Data
A CIP record for this book is available from the British Library
ISBN 978-1-84821-422-4

Contents

Preface

The energy performance in buildings is influenced by many factors, such as ambient weather conditions, building structure and characteristics, occupants and their behaviors, operation of sublevel components like heating, ventilation and air-conditioning systems. These complex properties make the prediction, analysis or fault detection/diagnosis of building energy consumption very difficult to perform accurately.

This book focuses on up-to-date data mining and machine-learning methods to solve these problems. This book first presents a review of recently developed models for solving prediction, analysis or fault detection/diagnosis of building energy consumption, including detailed and simplified engineering methods, statistical methods and artificial intelligence methods. Then, the methodology to simulate energy consumption profiles for single and multiple buildings is presented. Based on these datasets, support vector machine (SVM) models are trained and tested to do the prediction. The results from extensive experiments demonstrate high-prediction accuracy and robustness of these models. A recursive deterministic perceptron (RDP) neural network model is then used to detect and diagnose faulty building energy consumption. In the experiment, the RDP model shows a very high-detection ability. A new approach, based on the evaluation of RDP models, is also proposed here to diagnose faults. Since the selection of subsets of features significantly influences the performance of the model, the optimal features are selected based on the feasibility of obtaining them and on the scores they provide under the evaluation of two filter methods. Experimental results confirm the validity of the selected subsets and show that the proposed feature selection method guarantees the model accuracy and reduces the computational time. One challenge of predicting building energy consumption is to accelerate the model training when amounts of data are very large. To address this issue, this book proposes an efficient parallel implementation of SVMs based on the decomposition method. The parallelization is performed on the most time-consuming part of the training. The underlying parallelism is conducted with a shared memory Map-Reduce paradigm, making the system particularly suitable for multicore and multiprocessor systems. Experimental results show that our original implementation offers a high speedup compared to Libsvm, and it is superior to the state-of-the-art message passing interface (MPI) implementation of Pisvm in both computational time and storage requirement.

The aim of this book is to explain and illustrate, using concrete examples, the recent techniques of data mining and machine learning for solving prediction, analysis or fault detection/diagnosis of building energy consumption. We follow a didactic approach and gradually introduce mathematical and computing concepts where appropriate, and whenever the need arises to enhance understanding. This book is intended primarily for Master students in all fields of engineering concerned with building energy analysis. It may also interest any engineer working in the fields of data mining and knowledge discovery for energy management and energy efficiency. Portions of this book have been used, for a number of years by the authors, in seminars, keynotes and lectures on artificial intelligence at Wuhan University of Science and Technology (China), University Paris Saclay (France), Conservatoire National des Arts et Métiers (France), École Centrale des Arts et Manufactures (France), École Supérieure des Sciences et Technologies de l'Ingénieur de Nancy (France), University Duisburg-Essen (Germany), Chuo University (Japan), Doshisha University (Japan), Keio University (Japan) and University of Electro Communications (Japan).

Frédéric MAGOULÈS
Hai-Xiang ZHAO
November 2015

Introduction

The building energy conservation is a crucial topic in the energy field since buildings account for a considerable rate in the total energy consumption. The building's energy system is very complex, since it is influenced by many factors, such as ambient weather conditions, building structure and characteristics, occupants and their behaviors, the operation of sublevel components like heating, ventilating and air-conditioning (HVAC) systems. These complex properties make the prediction, or fault detection/diagnosis of building energy consumption very difficult to perform quickly and accurately.

Artificial intelligence models attract a lot of attention in solving complex problems. In this book, recently developed models for solving these problems, including detailed and simplified engineering methods, statistical methods and efficient artificial intelligence methods are reviewed. Then, energy consumption profiles are determined from measurements or are simulated for single and multiple buildings. Based on these datasets, support vector machine models are trained and tested to do the prediction. The results obtained on extensive experiments demonstrate high prediction accuracy and robustness of these models. Then, recursive deterministic perceptron (RDP) neural network model is used to detect and diagnose faulty building energy consumption. A new approach is proposed to diagnose faults. It is based on the evaluation of RDP models, each of which is able to detect an equipment fault. How to select subsets of features influences the model performance. The optimal features are here selected based on the feasibility of obtaining them and on the scores they provide under the evaluation of two filter methods. Experimental results confirm the validity of the selected subset and show that the proposed feature selection method can guarantee the model accuracy and reduce the computational time. Finally, one of the most difficult challenges of predicting building energy consumption is to accelerate model training when the dataset is very large. This book proposes an efficient parallel implementation of support vector machines (SVMs) based on the decomposition method for solving such problems. The parallelization is performed on the most time-consuming work of training, i.e. to update the gradient vector f. The inner problems are dealt with using a sequential minimal optimization solver. The underlying parallelism is conducted with a shared memory MapReduce paradigm, making the system particularly suitable to being applied to multicore and multiprocessor systems. Experimental results show that our implementation offers a high-speed increase compared to Libsvm, and it is superior to the state-of-the-art message passing interface (MPI) implementation Pisvm in both speed and storage requirement.

This book is organized as follows.

In Chapter 1, we first introduce the concept of building energy and present the background and motivation of this book, the problems and challenges. Then, we review the recently developed models and methods on predicting building energy consumption. These previous studies include solving all levels of energy analyzing problems with appropriate models, optimizing model parameters, treating inputs for better performance, simplifying the problems and comparing different models. Finally, we summarize the advantages and disadvantages of each model. Even if this chapter could not be fully exhaustive, it contains a heavy and detailed bibliography analysis and research history in the field of building energy analysis. As a result, this chapter can be omitted on a first reading, but the readers can refer to it for further reading or as an additional source of information when reading the following chapters.

Chapter 2 presents how to obtain historical energy consumption profiles. We list the common approaches and explain why in this book we choose to generate these data with EnergyPlus software. We develop a suitable interface to control EnergyPlus to simulate multiple buildings. The diversity of multiple buildings comes from different structure characteristics, envelope materials, occupancy, etc. Data uncertainties and calibration are also introduced in this chapter.

Chapter 3 introduces the principles of one of the most popular artificial intelligence models, namely the artificial neural network. We introduce the mechanism of this model and some widely used extensions, such as the feed forward neural network, radial basis neural network, recurrent neural network and recursive deterministic perceptron. At the end, we introduce some applications of these models. Chapter 3 also introduces another high-ability artificial intelligence model, namely the support vector machine, including the primal form, dual form, regularization and kernel method, plus extensions, including support vector regression (SVR), one-class, multiclass and transductive SVMs and applications. These models have demonstrated superiority in many sorts of applications, such as automatic text categorization, computational biology, image processing and so on.

Chapter 4 evaluates the SVR model in the application of predicting building energy consumption. First, we present several important issues in making experiments, including the schematic flow chart of an experiment, hardware and software environment, formatting data as needed, model selection and model performance evaluation. Then, we apply SVR to predict district heating in the winter season (evaluate on the last 2 days, train on remaining) and predict electricity consumption over one year (test on randomly selected 48 h, train on remaining). Next, we test the robustness of SVR. We train models on three datasets, January, January–April and January–August, and test the models on each remaining month. Then, we train the model on 99 buildings' consumption and test on a totally new building. Finally, we use the RDP neural network model to detect and diagnose faulty consumption in buildings. In the experiment, the RDP model shows very high-detection ability. A new approach is proposed to diagnose faults. It is based on the evaluation of several RDP models, each of which is able to detect a particular equipment fault. Our diagnostic method successfully diagnosed Chiller faults in the experiment. It is also able to sort the possible sources in decreasing order according to their possibilities of failure.

Chapter 5 presents a new feature selection approach for applying SVR in building energy consumption. The related work, algorithm and implementation are explained. Extensive experiments are performed to prove the validity of this method. The features are selected according to their feasibility in practice and usefulness to the predictor. The last criterion is evaluated under two filter methods: the gradient-guided feature selection and the correlation coefficients. To evaluate the proposed method, we use three training datasets to evaluate performance change of the model before and after feature selection. Experimental results show that the selected subset can provide competitive predictors. The number of features is reduced without losing model performance, making the model easier to use in practice. Performance improvement is also achieved in some cases. For instance, with both radial basis function and polynomial kernel on the data from 50 buildings, the model accuracy increases and the learning cost apparently decreases. This work serves as the first guide for selecting an optimal subset of features when applying machine learning methods for the prediction of building energy consumption.

Chapter 6 proposes an original parallel algorithm for SVC and SVR, which is especially suitable to multicore systems. We present the related work, decomposition quadratic problem (QP) solver, implementation details and comparative experiments on five benchmark datasets for SVC and result analysis. Then, we introduce parallel SVR and its application to building energy prediction. Our proposed method is based on a decomposition method. The variables are optimized iteratively. The parallelism is programmed in the simple, yet pragmatic programming framework MapReduce. A shared cache is designed to store kernel matrix columns. This implementation is especially suitable to multicore and multiprocessor systems. We have tested both SVC and SVR in extensive experiments. The results show that our new approach is very efficient in solving large-scale problems. It achieves high speedup with regard to the sequential implementation. The results also show superior performance of our implementation over a state-of-the-art parallel one in both training speed and memory requirement.

This book concludes by summarizing the innovative methods proposed and investigating the future of building energy analysis.

Overview of Building Energy Analysis

1.1. Introduction

In Europe, buildings account for 40% of total energy use and 36% of total CO_2 emission [EUR 10]. Figure 1.1 shows the annual energy consumption of each sector over 20 years from 1990 to 2009 in France. The part of industry decreased from 30% to 25%, and that of transport was stable around 30%. However, the usage of residential tertiary increased from 37% to 41%. We can see an increasing ratio of the building energy consumption during these years, and we can expect that the ratio will continue to increase in the future. The prediction of energy use in buildings is therefore significant for improving the energy performance of buildings, leading to energy conservation and reducing environmental impact.

However, the energy system in buildings is quite complex, as the energy types and building types vary greatly. In the literature, the main energy forms considered are heating/cooling loads, hot water and electricity consumption. The most frequently considered building types are offices, residential and engineering buildings, varying from small rooms to big estates. The energy behavior of a building is influenced by many factors, such as weather conditions, especially the dry bulb temperature, building construction and thermal property of the physical materials used, occupants and their behavior, sublevel components such as heating, ventilating and air conditioning (HVAC), and lighting systems.

Due to the complexity of the energy system, accurate consumption prediction is quite difficult. In recent years, a large number of approaches for this purpose, either elaborate or simple, have been proposed and applied to a broad range of problems. This research work has been carried out in the process of designing new buildings, operation or retrofit of contemporary buildings, varying from a building's subsystem analysis to regional or national level modeling. Predictions can be performed on the whole building or sublevel components by thoroughly analyzing each influencing factor or approximating the usage by considering several major factors. An effective and efficient model has always been the goal of the research and engineering community.

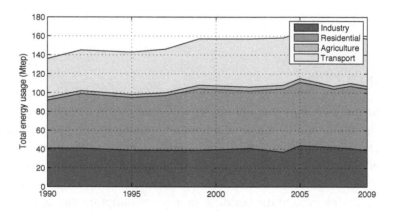

Figure 1.1. *Annual energy consumption in each sector of France (source: [COM 11])*

The following sections review the recent work related to the modeling and prediction of building energy consumption (more details can be found in [ZHA 12b] and reference therein). The methods used in this application include engineering, statistical and artificial intelligence methods. The most widely used artificial intelligence methods are artificial neural networks (ANNs) and support vector machines (SVMs). In 2003 and 2010, Krarti and Dounis provided two overviews of artificial intelligence methods in the application of building energy systems [KRA 03, DOU 10]. The following chapters of this book especially focus on the prediction applications. To even further enrich the content and provide the readers with a complete view of various prediction approaches, this section also reviews engineering and statistical methods. Moreover, there are also some hybrid approaches that combine some of the above models to optimize predictive performance (see [YAO 05, WAN 06, KAR 06] [LIA 07]). In the following, we describe the problems, models, related problems, such as data pre-/postprocessing, and the comparison of these models.

1.2. Physical models

The engineering methods use physical principles to calculate thermal dynamics and energy behavior for the whole building level or for sublevel components. They have been adequately developed over the past 50 years. These methods can be roughly classified into two categories, the detailed comprehensive methods and the simplified methods. The comprehensive methods use very elaborate physical functions or thermal dynamics to calculate precisely, step by step, the energy consumption for all components of the building with the building's and environmental information, such as external climate conditions, building construction, operation, utility rate schedule and HVAC equipment, as the inputs. In this section, we concentrate on the global view of models and applications, while the details of these computational processes are far beyond the purpose of this chapter. Readers may refer to [CLA 01] for more details. For HVAC systems, in particular, the detailed energy calculation is introduced in [MCQ 05]. The International Organization for Standardization (ISO) has developed a standard for the calculation of energy use for space heating and cooling for a building and its components [ISO 08].

Hundreds of software tools have been developed for evaluating energy efficiency, renewable energy, and sustainability in buildings, such as DOE-2, EnergyPlus, BLAST and ESP-r [SIM 11]. Some of them have been widely used for developing building energy standards and analyzing energy consumption and conservation measures of buildings. Surveys of these tools are performed in [ALH 01, CRA 08]. For readers' information, the U.S. Department of Energy (DOE) maintains a list of almost all the energy simulation tools [SIM 11], which is constantly updated.

Although these elaborate simulation tools are effective and accurate, in practice, there are some difficulties. Since these tools are based on physical principles, to achieve an accurate simulation, they require details of building and environmental parameters as input data. On the one hand, these parameters are unavailable to many organizations, for instance, the information on each room in a large building is always difficult to obtain. This lack of precise inputs will lead to a low accurate simulation. On the other hand, operating these tools normally requires tedious expert work, making it difficult to perform. For these reasons, some researchers have proposed simpler models to offer alternatives to certain applications.

Al-Homoud [ALH 01] reviewed two simplified methods. One is the degree day method in which only one index, degree day, is analyzed. This steady-state method is suitable for estimating small buildings' energy consumption where the envelope-based energy dominates. The other one is bin, also known as the temperature frequency method, which can be used to model large buildings where internally generated loads dominate or loads are not linearly dependent on outdoor/indoor temperature difference.

Weather conditions are important factors to determine building energy usage. These take many forms, such as temperature, humidity, solar radiation and wind speed, and vary over time. Certain studies are conducted to simplify weather conditions in building energy calculations. White and Reichmuth [WHI 96] attempted to use average monthly temperatures to predict monthly building energy consumption. This prediction is more accurate than standard procedures, which normally use heating and cooling degree days or temperature bins. Westphal and Lamberts [WES 04] predicted the annual heating and cooling load of non-residential buildings simply based on some weather variables, including monthly average of maximum and minimum temperatures, atmospheric pressure, cloud cover and relative humidity. Their results showed good accuracy on low mass envelope buildings, compared to elaborate simulation tools such as ESP, BLAST and DOE2.

As well as weather conditions, the building characteristic is another important yet complex factor in determining energy performance.

Yao and Steemers [YAO 05] developed a simple method of predicting a daily energy consumption profile for the design of a renewable energy system for residential buildings. The total building energy consumption was defined as the summation of several components: appliances, hot water and space heating. For each component, a specific modeling method was employed. For instance, to model electric appliances, they used the average end-use consumption from large amounts of statistical data. While modeling space heating demand, a simplified physical model was applied. Since the average value varies seasonally, this method predicts energy demand for one season at a time.

By adopting this divide-and-sum concept, Rice *et al.* [RIC 10] simplified each sublevel calculation to explain the system level building energy consumption. In the project "Updating the ASHRAE/ACCA Residential Heating and Cooling Load Calculation Procedures and Data" (RP-1199), Barnaby and Spitler [BAR 05b] proposed a residential load factor method, which is a simple method and can be done by hand. The load contributions from various sources were evaluated separately and then added up. Wang and Xu [WAN 06] simplified the physical characteristics of buildings to implement the prediction. For building envelopes, the model parameters were determined by using easily available physical details based on the frequency characteristic analysis. For various internal components, they used a thermal network of lumped thermal mass to represent the internal mass. A genetic algorithm was used to identify model parameters based on operation data. Yik *et al.* [YIK 01] used detailed simulation tools to obtain cooling load profiles for different types of buildings. A simple model, which is a combination of these detailed simulation results, was proposed to determine the simultaneous cooling load of a building.

Calibration is another important issue in building energy simulation. By tuning the inputs carefully, simulation can match the simulated energy behavior precisely with that of a specific building in reality. Pan *et al.* [PAN 07] summarized the calibrated simulation as one building energy analysis method and applied it to analyze the energy usage of a high-rise commercial building. After several repeated calibration steps, this energy model showed high accuracy in predicting the actual energy usage of the specified building. A detailed review of calibration simulation is provided in [RED 06]. Since calibration is a tedious and time-consuming work, we can see that doing accurate simulation using a detailed engineering method is of high complexity.

We note that there is no apparent boundary between the simplified and elaborate models. It is also possible to do simplified simulation with some comprehensive tools, such as EnergyPlus [CRA 01]. As suggested by Al-Homoud [ALH 01], if the purpose is to study trends, compare systems or alternatives, then simplified analysis methods might be sufficient. In contrast, for a detailed energy analysis of buildings and subsystems and lifecycle cost analysis, more comprehensive tools will be more appropriate [ALH 01].

1.3. Gray models

When the information of one system is partially known, we call this system a gray system. The gray model can be used to analyze building energy behavior when there is only incomplete or uncertain data.

In 1999, Wang *et al.* [WAN 99] applied a gray model to predict the building heat moisture system. The predicting accuracy is fairly high. Guo *et al.* [GUO 11] used an improved gray system to predict the energy consumption of heat pump water heaters in residential buildings. They evaluated the influence of a data sample interval in the prediction accuracy and found that the best interval is 4 weeks. This model requires little input data and the prediction error is within a normal range. Zhou *et al.* [ZHO 08] did on-line prediction of the cooling load by integrating two weather prediction modules into a simplified building thermal load model, which is developed in [WAN 06]: one is the temperature/relative humidity prediction, which is achieved by using a modified gray model, the other is solar radiation prediction, which is achieved using a regression model. Experimental results showed that the performance of the simplified thermal network model is improved as long as the predicted weather data from the first module are used in the training process.

1.4. Statistical models

Statistical models have been widely considered for building energy, including regression models, such as autoregressive model with eXtra inputs (ARX), autoregressive integrated moving average (ARIMA), autoregressive integrated moving average with eXtra inputs (ARIMAX) and conditional demand analysis (CDA).

Statistical regression models simply correlate the energy consumption or energy index with the influencing variables. These empirical models are developed from historical performance data, which means that before training the models, we need to collect enough historical data. Much research on regression models has been carried out on the following problems. The first is to predict the energy usage over simplified variables such as one or several weather parameters. The second is to predict a useful energy index. The third one is to estimate important parameters of energy usage, such as total heat loss coefficient, total heat capacity and gain factor, which are useful in analyzing thermal behavior of building or sublevel systems.

In some simplified engineering models, the regression is used to correlate energy consumption with the climatic variables to obtain an energy signature [BAU 98, WES 99, PFA 05]. Bauer and Scartezzini [BAU 98] proposed a regression method to handle both heating and cooling calculations simultaneously by dealing with internal as well as solar gains. Ansari *et al.* [ANS 05] calculated the cooling load of a building by adding up the cooling load of each component of the building envelope. Each sublevel cooling load is a simple regression function of temperature difference between inside and outside. Dhar *et al.* [DHA 98, DHA 99] modeled heating and cooling load in commercial buildings with outdoor dry bulb temperature as the only weather variable. A new temperature-based Fourier series model was proposed to represent nonlinear dependence of heating and cooling loads on time and temperature. If humidity and solar data are also available, they suggested using the generalized Fourier series model since it has more engineering relevance and higher prediction ability. Also considering dry bulb temperature as the single variable for model developing, Lei and Hu [LEI 09] evaluated regression models for predicting energy savings from retrofit projects of office buildings in a hot summer and cold winter region. They showed that a single variable linear model is sufficient and practical to model the energy use in hot and cold weather conditions. Ma *et al.* [MA 10] integrated multiple linear regression and self-regression methods to predict monthly power energy consumption for large-scale public buildings. In the work of Cho *et al.* [CHO 04], the regression model was developed on 1 day, 1 week and 3 month measurements, leading to the prediction error in the annual energy consumption of 100%, 30% and 6%, respectively. These results show that the length of the measurement period strongly influences the temperature-dependent regression models.

Concerning the prediction of the energy index, Lam *et al.* [LAM 10] used principle component analysis (PCA) to develop a climatic index Z with regard to global solar radiation and dry and wet bulb temperature. They found that Z has the same trend as simulated cooling load, HVAC, and building energy use. This trend was obtained from the analysis of correlation by a linear regression analysis. The model was developed based on the data from 1979 to 2007. Ghiaus [GHI 06] developed a robust regression model to correlate the heating loss on the dry bulb temperature by using the range between the first and the third quartile of the quantile–quantile plot, which gives the relation of these two variables.

Jiménez and Heras [JIM 05] used ARX to estimate the U and g values of building components. Kimbara *et al.* [KIM 95] developed an ARIMA model to implement on-line prediction. The model was first derived on the past load data, and was then used to predict load profiles for the next day. ARIMAX model has also been applied to some applications, such as predicting and controlling the peak electricity demand for commercial buildings [HOF 98] and predicting the power demand of the buildings [NEW 10]. In [NEW 10], Newsham and Birt put a special emphasis on the influence of occupancy, which can apparently increase the accuracy of the model.

Aydinalp-Koksal and Ugursal [AYD 08] suggested considering a regression-based method, called CDA, when we predict national level building energy consumption. In their experimental comparisons, CDA showed accurate predicting ability as good as neural networks and engineering methods, but that was easier to develop and use. However, the drawback of the CDA model was the lack of detail and flexibility, and it required a large amount of input information. CDA was also employed in the early work for analyzing residential energy consumption [LAF 94].

1.5. Artificial intelligence models

1.5.1. *Neural networks*

ANNs are the most widely used artificial intelligence models in the application of building energy prediction. This type of model is good at solving nonlinear problems and is an effective approach to this complex application. In the past 20 years, researchers have applied ANNs to analyze various types of building energy consumption in a variety of conditions, such as heating/cooling load, electricity consumption, sublevel components operation and optimization, and estimation of usage parameters. In this section, we review some past research and put them into groups according to the applications dealt with. Additionally, model optimization, such as the preprocessing of input data and comparisons between ANNs and other models, are highlighted at the end.

In 2006, Kalogirou [KAL 06] made a brief review of the ANNs in energy applications in buildings, including solar water heating systems, solar radiation, wind speed, air flow distribution inside a room, prediction of energy consumption, indoor air temperature and HVAC system analysis.

Kalogirou *et al.* [KAL 97] used back propagation neural networks to predict the required heating load of buildings. The model was trained on the consumption data of 225 buildings, which vary largely from small spaces to big rooms. Ekici and Aksoy [EKI 09] used the same model to predict building heating loads in three buildings. The training and testing datasets were calculated by using the finite difference approach of transient state one-dimensional heat conduction. Olofsson *et al.* [OLO 98] predicted the annual heating demand of a number of small single family buildings in the north of Sweden. Later, Olofsson and Andersson [OLO 01] developed a neural network that makes long-term energy demand (the annual heating demand) predictions based on short-term (typically from 2 to 5 weeks) measured data with a high prediction rate for single family buildings.

In [YOK 09], Yokoyama *et al.* used a back propagation neural network to predict cooling demand in a building. In their work, a global optimization method called modal trimming method was proposed for identifying model parameters. Kreider *et al.* [KRE 95] reported results of a recurrent neural network on hourly energy consumption data to predict building heating and cooling energy needs in the future, knowing only the weather and time stamp. Based on the same recurrent neural network, Ben-Nakhi and Mahmoud [BEN 04] predicted the cooling load of three office buildings. The cooling load data from 1997 to 2000 was used for model training and the data for 2001 was used for model testing. Kalogirou [KAL 00] used neural networks for the prediction of the energy consumption of a passive solar building where mechanical and electrical heating devices are not used. Considering the influence of weather on the energy consumption in different regions, Yan and Yao [YAN 10] used a back propagation neural network to predict a building's heating and cooling load in different climate zones represented by heating degree day and cooling degree day. The neural network was trained with these two energy measurements as parts of input variables.

In the application of building electricity usage prediction, an early study [JOI 92] has successfully used neural networks for predicting hourly electricity consumption as well as chilled and hot water for an engineering center building. Nizami and Al-Garni [JAV 95] tried a simple feed-forward neural network to relate the electric energy consumption to the number of occupants and weather data. González and Zamarreño [GON 05] predicted short-term electricity load with a special neural network, which feeds back part of its outputs. In contrast, Azadeh *et al.* [AZA 08] predicted the long-term annual electricity consumption in energy intensive manufacturing industries and showed that the neural network is very applicable to this problem when energy consumption shows high fluctuation. Wong *et al.* [WON 10] used a neural network to predict energy consumption for office buildings with day-lighting controls in subtropical climates. The outputs of the model include daily electricity usage for cooling, heating, electric lighting and total building.

ANNs are also used to analyze and optimize sublevel components' behavior, mostly for HVAC systems. Hou *et al.* [HOU 06a] predicted air conditioning load in a building, which is a key to the optimal control of the HVAC system. Lee *et al.* [LEE 04] used a general regression neural network to detect and diagnose faults in a building's air handling unit. Aydinalp *et al.* [AYD 02] showed that the neural network can be used to estimate appliance, lighting and space cooling (ALC) energy consumption, and it is also a good model to estimate the effects of the socioeconomic factors on this consumption in the Canadian residential sector. In their follow-up work, neural network models were developed to successfully estimate the space and domestic hot water heating energy consumptions in the same sector [AYD 04].

In [BEN 02] [BEN 04], general regression neural networks were used for air conditioning set-back controlling, and for optimizing HVAC thermal energy storage in public and office buildings. Yalcintas *et al.* [YAL 05] used neural networks to predict chiller plant energy use of a building in a tropical climate. Later, they used a three-layer feed-forward neural network to predict energy savings in an equipment retrofit [YAL 08]. Gouda *et al.* [GOU 02] used a multilayered feed-forward neural network to predict internal temperature with easily measurable inputs, which include outdoor temperature, solar irradiance, heating valve position and the building indoor temperature.

Building energy performance parameters can be estimated by neural networks. In [OLO 99, OLO 02, LUN 02, LUN 04], the authors estimated the total heat loss coefficient, the total heat capacity and the gain factor, which are important for a reliable energy demand forecast. The method is based on an analysis of a neural network model that is trained on simple data, the indoor/outdoor temperature difference, the supplied heat and the available free heat. Kreider *et al.* [KRE 95] reported results of recurrent neural networks on hourly energy consumption data. They also reported results on finding the thermal resistance, R, and thermal capacitance, C, for buildings from networks trained on building data. Zmeureanu [ZME 02] proposed a method using the general regression neural networks to evaluate the coefficient of performance of existing rooftop units. Yalcintas presented an ANN-based benchmarking technique for building energy in tropical climates, focused on predicting a weighted energy use index. The selected buildings are of a wide variety [YAL 06, YAL 07].

The input data for the model training can be obtained from on-site measurement, survey, billing collection or simulation. The raw data may have noisy or useless variables, therefore it can be cleaned and reduced before model development. There is much research concerning the data preprocessing technologies. González and Zamarreño [GON 05] predicted short-term electricity load by using two phases of neural networks. The first layer predicts climatic variables, while the second predicts energy usage, which takes the outputs of the first layer as inputs. The same two-phase technology was also used by Yokoyama *et al.* in predicting cooling load [YOK 09]. The trend and periodic change were first removed from data, and then the converted data was used as the main input for the model training. Additional inputs, including air temperature and relative humidity, were considered to use predicted values. Their effects on the prediction of energy demand were also investigated in this work.

Ben-Nakhi and Mahmoud [BEN 04] predicted the cooling load profile of the next day, and the model was trained on a single variable, outside dry bulb temperature. Ekici and Aksoy [EKI 09] predicted building heating loads without considering climatic variables. The networks were trained by only three inputs, transparency ratio, building orientation and insulation thickness. Kreider and Haberl [KRE 94] predicted the nearest future with the input of nearest past data. For predicting far future, they used recurrent neural networks. Yang *et al.* [YAN 05] used accumulative and sliding window methods to train neural networks for the purpose of on-line building energy prediction. Sliding windows constrained input samples in a small range.

Olofsson *et al.* [OLO 98] used PCA to reduce the variable dimension before predicting the annual heating demand. In their later work, they achieved long-term energy demand prediction based on short-term measured data [OLO 01]. Kubota *et al.* [KUB 00] used a genetic algorithm for the variable extraction and selection on measured data, and then fuzzy neural networks were developed for the building energy load prediction. Here, the variable extraction means translating original variables into meaningful information that is used as input in the fuzzy inference system. Hou *et al.* [HOU 06a] integrated rough sets theory and a neural network to predict an air conditioning load. Rough sets theory was applied to find relevant factors influencing the load, which were used as inputs in a neural network to predict the cooling load. Kusiak *et al.* [KUS 10] predicted the daily steam load of buildings by a neural network ensemble with five multilayer perceptrons (MLPs) methods since, in several case studies, it outperforms nine other data mining algorithms, including classification and regression trees (CART), CHAID, exhaustive Chi-squared automatic interaction detection (CHAID), boosting tree, multivariate adaptive regression (MARS) splines, random forest, SVM, MLP and k-nearest neighbors (k-NN). A correlation coefficient matrix and the boosting tree algorithm were used for variable selection. Karatasou *et al.* [KAR 06] studied how statistical procedures can improve neural network models in the prediction of hourly energy loads. The statistical methods, such as hypothesis testing, information criteria and cross validation, were applied in both input preprocessing and model selection. Experimental results demonstrated that the accuracy of the prediction is comparable to the best results reported in the literature.

The outputs of neural networks may not be exactly what we expected; Kajl *et al.* proposed a fuzzy logic to correct the outputs by postprocessing the results of neural networks. The fuzzy assistant allows the user to determine the impact of several building parameters on the annual and monthly energy consumption [KAJ 96, KAJ 97].

Some comparisons between neural network and other prediction models were performed in the literature. Azadeh *et al.* [AZA 08] showed that the neural network was very applicable to the annual electricity consumption prediction in manufacturing industries where energy consumption has a high fluctuation. It is superior to the conventional nonlinear regression model through analysis of variance. Aydinalp *et al.* [AYD 02] showed that neural networks can achieve higher prediction performance than engineering models in estimating ALC energy consumption and the effects of socioeconomic factors on this consumption in the Canadian residential sector. Later, ANN was compared with the CDA method in [AYD 08]. From this work, we see that CDA has a high ability to solve the same problem as the ANN model, while the former is easier to develop and use. Neto [NET 08] compared the elaborate engineering method with neural network model for predicting building energy consumption. Both models have shown high prediction accuracy, while ANN is slightly better than the engineering model in the short-term prediction.

1.5.2. *Support vector machines*

SVMs are increasingly used in research and industry. They are highly effective models in solving nonlinear problems even with small quantities of training data. Many studies of these models were conducted on building energy analysis in the past 5 years.

Dong *et al.* [DON 05a] first applied SVMs to predict the monthly electricity consumption of four buildings in the tropical region. Three-year data were trained and the derived model was applied to 1-year data to predict the landlord utility in that year. The results showed good performances of SVMs on this problem.

Lai *et al.* [LAI 08] applied this model on 1-year electricity consumption of a building. The variables include climate variations. In their experiments, the model was derived from 1-year performance and then tested on 3-month behavior. They also tested the model on each daily basis dataset to verify the stability of this approach during short periods. In addition, they added perturbation manually to a certain part of the historical performance and used this model to detect the perturbation by examining the change in the contributing weights.

Li *et al.* [LI 09] used SVMs to predict the hourly cooling load of an office building. The performance of the support vector regression is better than the conventional back propagation neural networks. Hou and Lian [HOU 09] also used SVMs for predicting the cooling load of the HVAC system. The result shows that SVMs are better than the ARIMA model.

Li *et al.* [LI 10a] predicted the annual electricity consumption of buildings by back propagation neural networks, radial basis function neural networks, general regression neural networks and SVMs. They found that general regression neural networks and SVMs were more applicable to this problem compared to other models. Furthermore, SVM showed the best performance among all prediction models. The models were trained on the data of 59 buildings and tested on nine buildings.

Liang and Du [LIA 07] presented a cost-effective fault detection and diagnosis method for HVAC systems by combining the physical model and a SVM. By using a four-layer SVM classifier, the normal condition and three possible faults can be recognized quickly and accurately with a small number of training samples. Three major faults are recirculation damper stuck, cooling coil fouling/block and supply fan speed decreasing. The indicators are the supply and mixed air temperatures, the outlet water temperature and the valve control signal.

Research was performed for pre- or postprocess model training. Lv *et al.* [LV 10] used PCA to reduce variables before training SVMs for predicting building cooling load. Li *et al.* [LI 10c] used an improved PCA, called kernel principal component analysis, before training SVMs to predict building cooling load. Li *et al.* [LI 10b] used a fuzzy C-mean clustering algorithm to cluster the samples according to their degree of similarity. Then, they applied a fuzzy membership to each sample to indicate its contribution to the model. In the postprocessing, Zhang and Qi [ZHA 09] applied Markov chains to do further interval forecasting after prediction of building heating load by SVMs.

1.6. Comparison of existing models

From the above description and analysis, it is obvious that a large number of calculations are needed to evaluate the building energy system, from subsystems to building level and even regional or national level. The reviewed research work is briefly summarized in Table 1.1, distinguished by considered problems and models, where we have omitted engineering methods because many of them can solve all of the problems. Each model has its own advantages in certain cases of applications.

Problems	Statistical	ANNs	SVMs
Heating/Cooling	[BAU 98, ANS 05] [DHA 99, DHA 98]	[KAL 97, EKI 09, OLO 98] [OLO 01, YAN 10, YOK 09] [KRE 95, BEN 04, KAL 00]	[LI 09, HOU 09] [LV 10, ZHA 09]
Electricity	[MA 10, HOF 98] [AZA 08, NEW 10]	[JOI 92, GON 05, AZA 08] [WON 10, AZA 08]	[DON 05a, LAI 08] [LI 10a]
Simplify	[DHA 98, DHA 99] [LEI 09]	[BEN 04, EKI 09, OLO 98] [KUB 00, KUS 10]	
System level	[ANS 05, LEI 09] [MA 10, CHO 04]		
Sub-system		[HOU 06a, LEE 04, AYD 02] [AYD 04, BEN 02, BEN 04] [YAL 05, YAL 08, GOU 02]	
Energy parameters	[JIM 05]	[OLO 99, OLO 02, LUN 02] [LUN 04, KRE 95, ZME 02]	
Energy index	[LAM 10, GHI 06]	[YAL 06, YAL 07]	
Data pre-/post- processing	[CHO 04, NEW 10]	[KAJ 96, KAJ 97, KRE 94] [YAN 05, KAR 06, KUS 10]	[LI 10c, LV 10] [ZHA 09, LI 10b]

Table 1.1. *Brief review of commonly used methods for the prediction of building energy consumption*

The engineering model shows large variations. Many considerations can be involved in developing this type of model. It can be a very elaborate, comprehensive model that is applicable for accurate calculations. In contrast, by adopting some simplifying strategies, it can become a lightweight model and is easy to develop while maintaining accuracy. A commonly accepted drawback of this detailed engineering model is that it is difficult to perform in practice due to its high complexity and the lack of input information.

The statistical model is relatively easy to develop but its major drawbacks when applied to building energy prediction are, most of the time, inaccuracy and lack of flexibility.

ANNs and SVMs are robust models at solving nonlinear problems, making them very applicable to building energy prediction. They can give highly accurate prediction as long as model selection and parameter settings are well performed. SVMs show an even more superior performance than ANNs in many cases [LI 10a]. The disadvantages of these two types of models are that they require sufficient historical performance data and are extremely complex compared to statistical models.

The comparative analysis of these commonly used models is summarized in Table 1.2. It is important to mention that this table is only a rough summary since each model has large uncertainty or variations.

Methods	Model Complexity	Easy to use	Running speed	Inputs needed	Accuracy
Elaborate Eng.	Fairly high	No	Low	Detailed	Fairly High
Simplified Eng.	High	Yes	High	Simplified	High
Statistical	Fair	Yes	Fairly high	Historical data	Fair
ANNs	High	No	High	Historical data	High
SVMs	Fairly high	No	Low	Historical data	Fairly high

Table 1.2. *Comparative analysis of commonly used methods for the prediction of building energy consumption*

1.7. Concluding remarks

This section has reviewed the recent work on prediction of building energy consumption. Due to the complexity of building energy behavior and the uncertainty of the influencing factors, many models were proposed for this application aiming at accurate, robust and easy-to-use prediction methods. Elaborate and simplified engineering methods, statistical methods and artificial intelligence, especially neural networks and SVMs, are widely used models. Research mainly concentrates on applying these models to new predicting problems, optimizing model parameters or input samples for better performance, simplifying the problems or model development and comparing different models under certain conditions. Each model is being developed and has its advantages and disadvantages, therefore it is difficult to say which one is better without a complete comparison under the same circumstances. However, artificial intelligence is developing rapidly, many new and more powerful technologies appearing in this field that may bring alternatives or even breakthroughs in the prediction of building energy consumption. Some of these new approach in artificial intelligence are detailed in the following chapters.

Data Acquisition for Building Energy Analysis

2.1. Introduction

As described in Chapter 1, the energy system in buildings is complex and contains many uncertainties. Therefore, accurate consumption data, especially the time series for each variable, are difficult to obtain. How to collect sufficient clean data is always an important concern in statistical analysis and model development. There are three common approaches to solve this problem. The first approach is to survey or do questionnaires from customers and collect data from building plan or energy providers. Data collected in these ways are always at the rough level, i.e. monthly or yearly consumption, or at the building level or even section level. The second approach is to do measurements in real buildings. This approach can provide energy performance in details, such as the hourly profile of a sensor. The third approach is to simulate these data numerically with some devoted software. Depending on the quality of these pieces of simulation software, this can provide us with clean consumption datasets the same as real consumption measurements.

This chapter will discuss how to collect real consumption data and how to perform simulation, providing the basic datasets that will be used in later chapters for developing models.

2.2. Surveys or questionnaires

Surveys or questionnaires are usually launched by utility companies, building management companies, energy analysis companies or government organizations. For instance, the benchmarking model developed in [YAL 07] uses electricity consumption data that were collected from a commercial buildings energy consumption survey database. This database was developed by the Energy Information Administration (EIA) of the U.S. Department of Energy, containing energy-related information of commercial buildings in 50 states of the United States. The data include building characteristics, and their energy consumption and expenses. Specially trained interviewers collect energy characteristics on the housing unit, usage patterns and household demographics. This information is combined with data from energy suppliers to these homes to estimate energy costs and usage for heating, cooling, appliances and other end-use information critical to meet future energy demand and improving efficiency and building design.

In order to represent the entire population of occupied housing units of the whole country, a multistage area probability design is used in sampling. It works as follows. Sample selection begins by randomly choosing counties. The selected counties are then subdivided into groups of census blocks called segments and a sample of segments is randomly drawn from the selected counties. Within each selected segment, a list of housing units is created by field listing. The final sample of housing units is randomly selected from the housing unit frame constructed from the selected area segments. The number of counties, segments, and housing units to be selected are carefully controlled so that this survey produces estimates of average energy consumption at specified levels of precision within the following geographic levels, called domains: national, census region, census division and individual states or group of states within census divisions.

In the household survey, trained interviewers use a standardized questionnaire to collect data from the selected housing units. The field interviewer records the householder's responses to the survey. Questions in the household survey are designed to collect energy-related characteristics of the housing unit, e.g. "What is the main fuel used for heating your home?", as well as energy usage patterns of the household members, e.g. "How often is your dishwasher used?". The interviewer records answers in his/her computer. Where respondents in rental housing units are less sure of their housing unit's energy characteristics, EIA uses the rental agent survey. Those data are collected by phone or in person from the unit's landlord or his/her representative.

All of the data collected from the household and rental agent surveys go through a series of rigorous statistical processes to ensure the highest possible data quality. These processes include editing, validation and quality control, and imputation of missing data.

After the household and rental agent surveys are completed, EIA conducts the energy supplier survey (ESS). This process is a follow-on mail survey required for energy companies that serviced housing units in the household survey. ESS gathers data on how much electricity, natural gas, fuel oil and propane were consumed by the sampled households during the reference year. It also asks for actual dollar amounts spent on these energy sources. Data from the survey follow the same quality assurance procedures as those from the household and rental agent surveys.

EIA produces estimates of end uses of energy by modeling the data from the household and energy supplier surveys. The flagship product of the renewable energy certificate system is the estimate of how much energy is used within the home for heating, cooling, refrigeration and other end uses. EIA estimates end-use consumption through a nonlinear statistical model applied to the collected data, which disaggregates total energy consumption into end-use components. These estimations make the survey uniquely important: it is the only survey that provides reliable, accurate and precise trend comparisons of energy consumption between households, housing types and areas of the country.

An energy audit identifies where energy is consumed and how much energy is consumed in an existing facility, building or structure. Information gathered from the energy audit can be used to introduce energy conservation measures or appropriate energy-saving technologies, such as electronic control systems, in the form of retrofits. An important part of energy auditing is energy accounting/bill auditing. Energy accounting is a process of collecting, organizing and analyzing energy data. For electricity accounts, the usage of data is normally tracked and should include metered kilowatt–hour consumption, metered peak demand, billed demand and rate schedules. Similar data are examined for heating fuel and water/sewer accounts. All of this information can be obtained by analyzing typical energy bills. Creating energy accounting records and performing bill audits can be done internally without hiring outside consulting firms. Also, while energy audits as a whole will identify excessive energy use and cost-effective conservation projects, bill auditing will assist in identifying errors in utility company bills and beneficial rate and service options. It could provide an excellent opportunity to generate savings without any capital investment.

Let us make an overview of a typical audit process. An energy audit team is established to organize and manage the process. The team should include the municipal business administrator, facilities manager and environmental and maintenance staff. The capabilities of these staff members should help determine the necessity of hiring outside experts. The expertise of an energy specialist, who generally has an architectural or engineering background, is required for a thorough audit. This specialist should be able to provide up-to-date knowledge of an energy-efficient plant and equipment as well as computer modeling skills for energy use and management.

Energy auditing evaluates the efficiency of all building components and systems that impact energy use. The audit process begins at the utility meters where the sources of energy coming into a building or facility are measured. Energy flow inputs and outputs for each fuel are then identified. These flows are measured and quantified into distinct functions or specific uses, then the function and performance of all building components and systems are evaluated. The efficiency of each of the functions is assessed, and energy and cost-saving opportunities are identified. At the end of the process, an energy audit report is prepared. The report should contain documentation of the use and occupancy of the audited buildings, as well as an assessment of the condition of the buildings and the associated systems and equipment. The report should also include recommendations on how to increase energy efficiency through improvements in operation and maintenance and installation of energy saving technologies and energy conservation measurements.

The best way to determine the appropriate type of audit is to look at the energy use index of the facility or buildings. There are three types of audit. The first is a walk-through audit. This is the least expensive. It involves an examination of the building or facility, including a visual inspection of each of the associated systems. Historic energy usage data are reviewed to analyze patterns of energy use and compare them with sector/industry averages or benchmarks for similar structures. The walk-through audit provides an initial estimate of potential savings and generates a menu of inexpensive savings options usually involving incremental improvements. Information from this level of audit also serves as a basis for determining if a more comprehensive audit will be needed. The second is standard audit. This involves a more comprehensive and highly detailed evaluation. Facilities, equipment, operational systems and conditions are assessed thoroughly, and on-site measurements and testing are conducted to arrive at a careful quantification of energy use, including losses. The energy efficiencies of the various systems are determined using accepted energy engineering computational techniques. Technical changes and improvements in each of the systems are analyzed to determine the corresponding potential energy and cost savings. In addition, the standard audit will include an economic analysis of the proposed technological improvements. The third is simulation on computers, which is discussed later in section 2.4.

2.3. Measurements

Some researchers use measurement data in their analysis. In the early work [KAL 00], the investigated building was a holiday home and the recorded variables were easily measurable, i.e. season, insulation conditions in all four walls, actual thickness where the heat transfer coefficient was constant and time of day. In [HOU 06a], the load prediction model was tested on the measurements of an HVAC system in service. In [LUN 04], the authors investigated 87 single-family buildings in Sweden. Fifteen thermocouples were used for measuring the temperatures in each house. Nine of them inside and six outside, providing the internal and external average temperatures, respectively. The data were recorded every second and averaged for minute intervals. The cost of measuring energy use within buildings is a nonlinear function of the sample size. In order to gather a sufficient variety of social parameters, a large number of houses will need to be measured. Methods are being established to make best use of the information collected. Some measurement practices are listed in the following.

Barley *et al.* [BAR 05a] proposed a procedure to provide a standard method for measuring and characterizing the energy performance of commercial buildings. The procedure determines the energy consumption, electrical energy demand and on-site energy production in existing commercial buildings of all types. The procedure is divided into two tiers to differentiate the resolution of the results and the amount of effort typically required to complete the procedure. Tier 1 gives monthly and annual results for the facility as a whole, based primarily on utility meter readings. Tier 2 yields time-series results (typically 15- or 60-min data, which should correspond to the electrical demand billing scheme, if applicable), in addition to monthly and annual results, itemized by the type of end use, based on submetering and a data acquisition system. With either Tier 1 or Tier 2, performance is measured for a period of 1 year to determine seasonal trends and annual totals. Typically, for a Tier 1 analysis of an existing building, such data have already been recorded on utility bills, so the procedure may be completed in a matter of days. For a Tier 1 analysis of a newly completed building, a 1-year waiting period will be necessary to collect the data. For a Tier 2 analysis, the measurement (which will take at least 1 year to complete) is part of the procedure.

The Household Energy End-Use Project (HEEP) is a long-term study with purpose of measuring and modeling the way how energy is used in New Zealand households [HEE 12]. The project is launched in 1995 with a pilot study and progressed to detailed data collection in 400 houses from throughout New Zealand. The sample includes households from large and small cities, urban and rural areas and both the North and South Islands from Kaikohe to Invercargill. Each house was monitored for about 11 months.

Two types of measurements are undertaken in HEEP: energy end-use measurement that records the energy consumption down to individual end uses (hot water, lighting, heating, cooking, etc.), and whole building energy measurement that measures the various energy flows into the building. Where possible the whole building energy measurement also includes the measurement of large energy end uses such as water heating. The experimental method for HEEP is intended to involve the measuring of energy use in at least 400 houses throughout the country. With 11 sets of end-use measuring equipment available, it is anticipated that 55 houses will be able to be measured at the end-use level over the 5 years of measurements. The remaining 345 houses will be monitored at the whole building energy level. The HEEP database is setup to a 10 min interval. Data from the loggers are aggregated from 1- and 2-min intervals to 10 min. End-use extraction will need to be undertaken on the raw, 1 and 2 min data with the 10 minutes end-use estimates being input into the HEEP database. With there being a variety of accuracy for data in the HEEP database, estimates of data accuracy would be useful to include within the database structure. With many determinants of energy use having a daily frequency (e.g. the temperature), an important analysis time interval is daily consumption information. Daily information will be the basis on which seasonal effects will be seen in the data.

Any data collection system makes an impact on the occupants of the house. In order to minimize this impact for the HEEP project, cabling is kept to a minimum. The measurement of total electrical, reticulated natural gas and liquefied petroleum gas usage within a building is achieved in the HEEP project with a separation between the sensor and the data capture and storage device (data logger). A consequence of this is that there is no central logging point within the house but instead each logger is independent. Modem communications are therefore not possible and regular visits are required to house the off-load data.

The sensors used for measuring electricity and gas are consumption sensors (energy for electricity and volume for gas) as opposed to rate-of-consumption sensors (power for electricity and flow for gas). The output of the consumption sensor is a pulse for each marginal unit of consumption. There is no time setting required as this is undertaken by the data capture device connected to the sensor. The sensor used to monitor electrical energy in houses is a static (solid state) watt–hour meter, as used by many power companies. The particular meter is a single phase Siemens S2A100S meter. These meters are manufactured in large quantities and consequently the meter is cheaper than dedicated kilowatt–hour transducers. This meter also incorporates a logging capacity; however, it is limited to half-hour intervals and is capable of only storing 1-week duration of data and thus is not suitable for anything other than basic monitoring tasks. The Siemens meter is installed on the meter board immediately following the power company meter. The small size of the Siemens meter (145 mm × 100 mm × 55 mm) frequently allows additional Siemens meters to be installed on the meterboard allowing additional large loads (such as the hot water cylinder) to be monitored. As the current sample region is largely urban (Wellington, Lower Hutt, Upper Hutt and Porirua City Council areas), there has not been a great need to monitor houses supplied with multiphase electricity. The measurement of reticulated gas involves interrupting the gas pipes to the house or to individual appliances to install Gallus 2000 G2.5 gas flow meters. The Gallus 2000 G2.5 is a standard tariff meter as used for the supply of natural gas to households. The Gallus meters have been fitted with a pulsed output providing a pulse for each 0.01 m^3 of gas delivered. The volume of gas delivered by the Gallus meter for flows between 0.03 and 4.0 m^3/hr is within a range of 1.5% of the reading. This range corresponds to a standard uncertainty in the volume measurement of 0.9% of the reading. The installation of additional gas meters within existing pipework can be an awkward and expensive task. The physical size of the meters (280 mm × 220 mm × 180 mm) restricts locations where the meters can be placed within the house. The use of bottled Liquefied Petroleum Gas (LPG) in New Zealand is considerable. There are approximately 400,000 portable LPG heaters in New Zealand. For the measurement of bottled LPG usage, the Gallus meter is also used. For portable LPG heaters, these meters are mounted on a board protruding from the back of the heater extending the depth of the heater by about 250 mm.

The output of the electricity and gas sensors are pulse signals. Pulse signals are easy to process as they can be converted into the digital domain easily. The logger used to capture and store the consumption information is a BRANZ pulse logger. The emphasis with these loggers was to develop a data collector specifically for this application rather than to develop a general purpose logger. By limiting the flexibility of the logger, it has been possible to extend many of the features compared with general purpose loggers.

As the HEEP database is set up as an evenly spaced time series, the number of pulses occurring within a preset interval is the basis of the stored information rather than the time between pulse events (such as recording the time between consecutive pulses). Up to four channels of pulse inputs can be recorded by the logger with each channel capable of recording 254 pulses per logging interval. This limitation of 254 pulses requires that the logging time interval is selected small enough to allow the storage of the power being monitored. For electricity, the maximum energy that can be recorded in each interval is 0.254 kWh. When a 1-min interval is used, the maximum power that can be monitored is 15.3 kW, and when a 2-min interval is used, the maximum power is halved to 7.65 kW. For gas, the greatest volume of gas that can be measured within an interval is 2.54 m^3. Consequently, the largest energy that can be recorded for an individual reading is approximately 29 kWh (104 MJ) for natural gas and 83 kWh (298 MJ) for LPG (the calorific values in section 4.3.1 have been used). The BRANZ pulse logger has 64 k of memory providing storage for approximately 59,000 readings. The length of time before the memory becomes full depends on the number of channels logged and time interval of the channels. For the HEEP monitoring, it is intended that the loggers be off-loaded on a monthly basis. The two modes used for the HEEP monitoring are one channel, 1-min logging and two channel, 2-min logging. Both these modes set the logger storage capacity to approximately 41 days.

The HEEP data collection also needs to account for the energy used in solid fuel appliances such as enclosed wood burners, open fires, coal burners and other such appliances. The number of dynamic parameters determining the energy output of solid fuel appliances is large. It is difficult to control or monitor many of these parameters outside the laboratory. The estimation of solid fuel energy therefore has a larger uncertainty than the other fuel types. The data collected on solid fuel includes information on the type of fuel loaded into the burner as well as measurements of surface temperatures of the burner. The occupants are asked to fill out a notebook when they use the burner. This notebook identifies the type and amount of fuel used as well as comments such as damper settings on the appliance. The surface temperature of the burner is recorded by a temperature data logger and provides an indication of how much heat is being delivered to the room.

With space heating being a large contribution to the energy use in New Zealand houses, additional information that adds to the understanding of space heating is important. An important parameter to the understanding of space heating is the temperature within the building. Indoor temperatures are determined by the occupants and the building. Data logger technology has advanced in recent years to allow for the measurement of indoor temperatures with a short time interval (10 or 15 min). These detailed temperature time series provide information on the effectiveness of the space heating systems as well as the dependence of the indoor temperatures on external conditions. Sensor placement is a critical issue for the measurement of indoor temperatures and this is currently under investigation in the HEEP project.

2.4. Simulation

The first two approaches, survey and measurement, aim at recording real consumption data. They usually take a very long time and run the risk of inaccuracy in practice. Many researchers prefer to use simulation methods instead of them. The computer simulation approach is less expensive and is often recommended for more complicated systems, structures or facilities. This involves using computer simulation software for prediction purposes, i.e. performance of buildings and systems, and consideration of effects of external factors, e.g. changes in weather and other conditions. With the computer simulation audit, a baseline related to a facility actual energy use is established, against which effects of system improvements are compared. This audit is often used for assessing the energy performance of new buildings based on different design configurations and equipment packages.

For instance, in [NET 08], the authors used EnergyPlus to simulate an administration building of the University of Sao Paulo (Brazil). They kept the building description and its internal loads as simple as possible in order to avoid overdetailed modeling. They chose the climate data and a set of parameters that briefly described the building: geometry, wall and window materials, lighting, equipment and occupancy schedules. The daily total energy consumption was recorded and compared with the actual measured data. It turns out that they are highly consistent. In the simulation period, i.e. from January to March 2005, 80% of the simulated energy demands came quite close to the measured one. In fact, as long as calibration is well performed, the simulation approach is possible to produce energy consumption data that approaches real profiles very closely [RED 06].

A procedure for simulation should provide instructions regarding the choice of software, time step, assumed building operating conditions, weather data and many other modeling parameters. Without guidelines for these choices, results may vary significantly. However, it may prove useful to apply the metrics defined here in a simulation analysis to facilitate a subsequent comparison of measured performance to simulated performance. There are a wild variety of programs that can be used to simulate building energy profiles, as listed in [SIM 11].

2.4.1. *Simulation software*

The popular and newly emerging pieces of building energy software are collected in "Building Energy Software Tools Directory". It provides information on more than 400 building software tools for evaluating energy efficiency, renewable energy and sustainability in buildings. The energy tools listed in this directory include databases, spreadsheets, component and system analyses, and whole-building energy performance simulation programs. A short description is provided for each tool along with other information including expertise required, users, audience, input, output, computer platforms, programming language, strengths, weaknesses, technical contact and availability. This directory is sponsored by the DOE. The DOE developed this directory because the Office of Building Technology, State and Community Program (BTS) develops software tools to help researchers, designers, architects, engineers, builders, code officials and others involved in the building lifecycle to evaluate and rank potential energy-efficiency technologies and renewable energy strategies in new or existing buildings. Many of the 50 tools in the first version released in August 1996 were sponsored by the DOE at some point in their lifecycle. Let us present some widely used software in the following:

– *DOE-2*: this is an hourly, whole-building energy analysis program calculating energy performance and lifecycle cost of operation. It can be used to analyze the energy efficiency of given designs or the efficiency of new technologies. Other uses of this software include utility demand side management, development and implementation of energy efficiency standards and compliance certification.

– *TRNSYS*: this is an energy simulation program whose modular system approach makes it a flexible tool. TRaNsient SYstem Simulation Program (TRNSYS) includes a graphical interface, a simulation engine and a library of components that range from various building models to standard HVAC equipment to renewable energy and emerging technologies. TRNSYS also includes a method for creating new components that do not exist in the standard package. This simulation package has been used for more than 30 years for HVAC analysis and sizing, multizone airflow analyses, electric power simulation, solar design, building thermal performance, analysis of control schemes, etc.

– *EnergyPlus*: EnergyPlus is a whole-building energy simulation program that engineers, architects and researchers use to model energy and water use in buildings. Modeling the performance of a building with EnergyPlus enables building professionals to optimize the building design to use less energy and water. EnergyPlus includes many innovative simulation capabilities: time-steps less than 1 hour, modular systems and plant integrated with heat balance-based zone simulation, multizone air flow, thermal comfort, water use, natural ventilation and photovoltaic systems. EnergyPlus is the succession of the well-known energy and load simulation tool BLAST and DOE-2.1E, maintained by DOE. Inheriting the capabilities and advantages of its two legacy programs, EnergyPlus is comprehensive in energy analysis and thermal simulation of complex building systems.

Figure 2.1 gives a brief overview of the structure of this simulation program. Given a user's description of a building, EnergyPlus calculates the heating and cooling loads that are necessary to maintain thermal control setpoints, conditions throughout a secondary HVAC system and coil loads, and the energy consumption of primary plant equipment as well as many other simulation details that are necessary to verify that the simulation is performed in the way that the actual building would do. This integrated solution provides more accurate space temperature prediction that is crucial for system and plant sizing, occupant comfort and occupant health calculations.

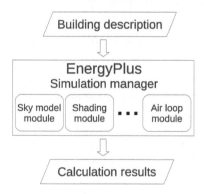

Figure 2.1. *Overview of EnergyPlus software*

2.4.2. *Simulation process*

In order to illustrate the simulation process on a concrete example, we describe in the following sections the simulation of energy consumption on one single building and on multiple buildings with EnergyPlus.

2.4.2.1. *Simulation details*

In order to test the model sufficiently, we simulate energy consumption data for both single and multiple buildings. All of these buildings are for office use and located in France. For each dataset, we record the total heating demand or total electricity consumption as the target. We also record dozens of variables as the features in the datasets. Each sample of the dataset is hourly consumption. Weather conditions are important factors that determine building's energy consumption. We suppose the simulated single building is located in an urban area, such as Paris-Orly, therefore the weather data in such a place is used as a part of inputs during the simulation. Other than the weather conditions, the inputs also contain the descriptions of buildings, occupants' behavior, etc. Since the inputs are in large quantity and there is no need to list them all, we put them into four categories as listed below, weather conditions, building structure characteristics, occupant behaviors and inner facilities and their schedules:

– weather conditions include dry bulb temperature, relative humidity, global horizontal radiation, wind speed, etc;

– building structure characteristics include shape, capacity, orientation, window/wall radio, fenestration/shading, building materials, thermal zones, etc.;

– occupants' behaviors include such as number of occupants, their leaving and entering time, thermal comfortable set points, ventilation, etc.;

– inner facilities and their schedules include such as lighting system, heating, ventilation and air conditioning, system, television, computer, etc.

The weather conditions are very complicated, since they vary over time and according to the location. Fortunately, the real recorded weather data for recent years is readily available. We chose them in our simulation. For example, when we want to simulate a building in Paris-Orly, we choose the weather data in this area as the inputs to EnergyPlus. The considered weather data includes dry bulb air temperature, relative humidity, wind speed, global horizontal radiation and ground temperature. To have an overview of their variations, the dry bulb air temperatures of the first 20 days in January and July are shown in Figure 2.2, and the relative humidity on the same days are shown in Figure 2.3. We can see many sudden changes in these curves.

In the following, we try to generate the consumption data of a single building initially in the heating season. Then, by modifying some alterable input parameters, we generate the consumption profiles for multiple buildings.

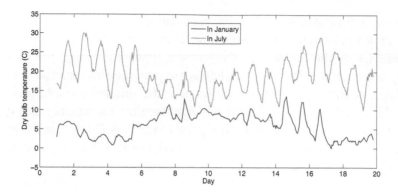

Figure 2.2. *Dry bulb temperature in the first 20 days
of January and July. For a color version of this figure, see
www.iste.co.uk/magoules/mining.zip*

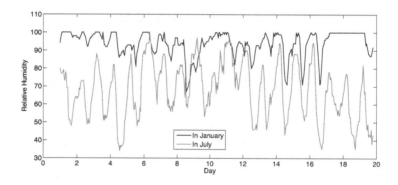

Figure 2.3. *Relative humidity in the first 20 days of January and July.
For a color version of this figure, see
www.iste.co.uk/magoules/mining.zip*

2.4.2.2. *Simulation of one single building*

The first building is simulated in the heating season, i.e. from November 1 to March 31. The description of this building is shown in Table 2.1. In order to show more details, we extract the materials of surfaces, shown in Table 2.2. These materials determine the thermal behavior of the building envelope and significantly influence the total energy consumption. Descriptions of these materials can be found in the documents of EnergyPlus [ENE 11].

For the sake of simplicity, we suppose there is only one floor and one room in this building. Since it is in the heating season, the energy consumed in this building mainly comes from three sources: the district heating that is used to keep the inside temperature at a constant level, electricity plants that are used mostly on working days and hot water for office use. For the walls in each orientation, there are several construction layers due to thermal considerations. This explains why there are three materials in the wall structure as presented in Table 2.2. The same applies for the roof that is composed of three materials. The open/close time of the building and schedules of the inner equipment are carefully set as for normal office purposes in France.

Parameters	Values
Location	Paris-orly, City
Duration	From November 1st to March 31st
Time Step	15 min
Building Shape	Rectangle
Structure	Length:11 m, Width:10 m, Ceiling Height:4 m, North axis:10°
Fenestration Surface	14 m^2 for each wall
Thermal Zones	1
People	14
Air Infiltration	0.0348 m^3/s
Heating Type	District Heating
Cooling Type	HVAC windowAirCondioner
Other Facilities	Light, Water heater

Table 2.1. *Description of a single building (in metric units)*

Structures	Material's name	Thickness (m)	Conductivity (W/mK)
Wall	1IN Stucco	0.0253	0.6918
	8IN Concrete HW	0.2033	1.7296
	Wall Insulation	0.0679	0.0432
Ground	MAT-CC05 8 HW CONCRETE	0.2032	1.311
Roof	Roof Membrane	0.0095	0.16
	Roof Insulation	0.1673	0.049
	Metal Decking	0.0015	45.006
Windows	Theoretical Glass [117]	0.003	0.0185

Table 2.2. *Building materials used in simulation*

During the simulation, the output is damped hourly. There are several output files in EnergyPlus, and we extract the time series data. Postprocessing of these data is required for further analysis, including reformatting the data into the form required by the analyzing tools. The consumption target is district heating demand or total electricity consumption. Meanwhile, we take 25 variables as features. They are listed in the following category:

– day type indicates if the current day is a holiday or a normal working day;

– weather conditions;

– zone mean air temperatures;

– infiltration volume;

– heat gain through each window;

– heat gain through lights;

– heat gain from people;

– zone internal total heat gain.

For readers to understand what the consumption profile looks like, we take the target, electricity consumption in the whole month of November, as an example, as shown in Figure 2.4. Intuitively, the hourly consumption varies periodically. In the middle of one day, around 12 o'clock, the electricity requirement reaches maximum, while at night it is at the lowest level. We also see that at the weekends, holidays and national days (11 November, date of the Armistice 1918), there is a low energy demand.

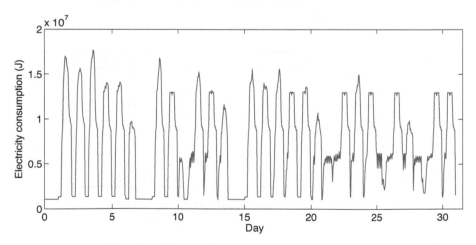

Figure 2.4. *Hourly electricity consumptions of the single building in the first simulation month (November)*

2.4.2.3. *Simulation of multiple buildings*

In order to generate data for more buildings, we suppose that all buildings are of the same type, specifically, for office use, and have analogous characteristics. In our approach, the previously used input file is divided into two parts. The first part is called the alterable part, containing the parameters that are probably different for each building, such as structure characteristics, location, weather conditions, number of occupants, etc. Their values are obtained by stochastic methods, but should be in a reasonable domain. The second is the stable part where the parameters for each building are always the same, for instance, the schedules of inner electrical plants that each building shares since they are all for the same office use. When a new building is required, we first update the alterable part to make it specific to this building, then combine it with the stable part to create the final input file for EnergyPlus. After successfully simulating one building, the program goes back to update the alterable part for simulating the next one. This process is repeated until the predefined number of buildings is finished. In a parallel environment, buildings are simulated in parallel; on multicore computers, one building is allocated to one core.

To have an overview of the multiple buildings' consumption, we randomly choose one building and draw its consumption together with the consumption of the first building (simulated in Figure 2.4) as shown in Figure 2.5. We can see that the basic trends of these two sequences are the same, but at some peak points, they are very different in value.

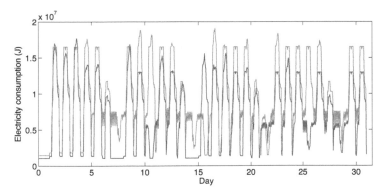

Figure 2.5. *Hourly electricity consumptions of two buildings in November. For a color version of this figure, see www.iste.co.uk/magoules/mining.zip*

2.5. Data uncertainty

Data generated from the sensor network is usually what is commonly called uncertain data or raw data, i.e. incomplete, imprecise, with noisy and even misleading values. All measurements contain some uncertainty generated through systematic or random error. For instance, uncertain data streams have been observed in environmental monitoring sensor networks, radio frequency identification networks, global positioning systems (GPS), camera sensor networks and radar sensor networks. As such raw data streams are fed into processing systems to support tracking and monitoring applications, the results to the end applications are often of unknown quality. Acknowledging and handling the uncertainty of data is of importance when reporting the results of scientific investigation.

Uncertainties can be reduced in careful methodology by correcting systematic error and minimizing random error. Figure 2.6 shows common uncertainties in data including missing points, outliers and noisy values that are common in raw datasets. In the preprocessing step, for missing points, one simple handling method consists of removing them from the data. This would not influence the model performance as long as the data size is large. Another consideration consists of restoring these points using interpolation.

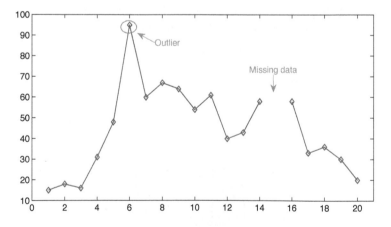

Figure 2.6. *Data uncertainty*

Outliers are defined as data values that are dramatically different from other data or have values that appear to be inconsistent with the other data. They may be due to measurement error, or may represent significant features in the data. Identifying outliers, and deciding what to do with them, depends on an understanding of the data and its source. One method for identifying outliers is to look for values more than a certain number of standard deviations from the mean. The threshhold is determined depending on the specific requirement of application. The outliers can be removed or corrected. Removing an outlier has a greater effect on the standard deviation than on the mean of the data. Deleting one such point leads to a smaller new standard deviation, which might result in making some remaining points appear to be outliers.

Noise is very common in raw data, it shows random variations about expected values. You may want to smooth the data to reveal its main features before building a model. The smoothing algorithm results in values that are better estimates of expected values because the noise has been reduced. Smoothing estimates the center of the distribution of response values at each value of the predictor. It invalidates a basic assumption of many fitting algorithms, namely, that the errors at each value of the predictor are independent. Accordingly, we can use smoothed data to identify a model, but avoid using smoothed data to fit a model. The common algorithms for smoothing data are moving average filter and discrete filter.

2.6. Calibration

Calibration compares the results of the simulation with real measured data and tunes the simulation parameters until the results closely match the real consumption data. No matter what model is used, calibration of simulation is necessary and crucial for the accuracy and usability of building energy simulation.

A large amount of research work has been carried out within this topic. Norford et al. [NOR 94] discussed the major sources of the wide discrepancy between predicted and actual energy use and in the process of simulation and calibration, they formulated calibration guidelines and developed insights that may be of use to others. Pedrini et al. [PED 02] employed the method of simulation and calibration to model more than 15 office buildings in Brazil; Chimack [CHI 01] used the calibrated DOE-2 model to determine the peak cooling loads and do energy assessment of a 107-year-old science museum; Yoon et al. [YOO 03] developed a systematic method using a "base load analysis approach" to calibrate a building energy performance model with a combination of monthly utility billing data and submetered data in large buildings in Korea.

Calibrated simulation is well defined in the ASHRAE Guideline 14-2002: Measurement of Energy and Demand Savings [ASH 02]. Calibrated simulation is an appropriate method to measure and determine energy and demand savings of energy conservation measurement under the conditions, e.g. when whole-building metered electrical data are not available or when savings cannot be determined by measurements or when measures interact with other building systems but it is difficult to isolate the savings, etc. Calibrated simulation is also very useful for facility professionals who can benefit from the availability of a model to explore energy saving potentials as well as energy conservation measurement impacts. However, calibrated simulation cannot be used under some conditions, e.g. when measures can be analyzed without simulation, or when buildings or HVAC systems cannot be readily simulated, or when the resources are not sufficient and so on. The calibrated simulation approach has the following steps:

– *produce a calibrated simulation plan*: in the preparation of a calibrated simulation plan, the baseline scenario and post-retrofit scenario have to be specified, the simulation software has to be selected and the tolerances of calibration indices have to be checked;

– *collect data*: data include building plans (building geometry and construction materials), operating schedules, historical utility data (a minimum of 12 months, hourly data if available), information of building system components (lighting systems, plug loads, HVAC systems, building envelope and thermal mass, building occupants, other major energy-using loads) and weather data (a typical year and a specific year). On-site surveys, interviews, spot and short-term measurements, etc., could be appropriate methods to collect these data and information;

– *input data and run model*: the best guide to inputting data into a model is the user manual of the simulation software selected by the simulator. In order to minimize the simulation error, the following data should be checked as input or output: (1) building orientation, (2) HVAC system zoning, (3) external surface characteristics, (4) lighting and plug load power densities and operating schedules, (5) HVAC system characteristics and operating schedules and (6) plant equipment characteristics;

– *calibration of simulation model*: one of the following three approaches must be selected for calibration: (1) comparing model monthly usage predictions to monthly utility bill data, (2) comparing model monthly usage predictions to monthly utility bill data in combination with comparing model subsystem usage predictions to measured hourly data, and (3) comparing model hourly usage predictions to hourly utility bill data;

– *refine model*: if the statistical indices calculated during the previous step indicate that the model is not sufficiently calibrated, revise the model inputs, run the model and compare its prediction to the measured data again;

– *calculate energy and demand savings.*

Both the baseline model and the post-retrofit model are run to calculate the energy and demand savings of each energy conservation measurement.

2.7. Concluding remarks

Sufficient and precise consumption data is important for model evaluation. Unfortunately, it is difficult to obtain in practise. Simulation is a popular approach in the academic community and is becoming more and more used in industry. Since weather conditions are available and elaborate calibration can guarantee accuracy, we choose this approach in the following. When preparing the inputs of EnergyPlus, we carefully set the parameters according to real situations in France in order to make the simulated building more like the real one.

In the above multiple-building generation, all buildings are for office use, so their consumption might be similar. With our approach, it is quite easy to simulate totally different buildings, such as residential, commercial or teaching buildings, which could vary from small spaces to large estates. The sublevel components can also be recorded in the simulation. However, since our aim is to develop high-performance statistical models, there is no need to simulate all of these building types.

The data acquisition could be done either in-house or by use of outside consultants, depending on the level of audit required and availability of expertise and resources. Internal staff could carry out the walk-through audit. When outside help from a consultant, contractor or independent energy auditor is needed, the search and selection should be done carefully to get the best and most reliable service. Data preprocessing can provide clean data for model development while handling uncertainties such as missing samples, outliers and noisy.

To make the data more likely to reflect reality, careful calibration is necessary in every simulation method. Engineers should choose the suitable method according to what source they have and what granularity the application requires.

Artificial Intelligence Models

3.1. Introduction

Artificial intelligence (AI) is a branch of computer science with the aim of making machines capable of reasoning and perception. This overall objective is pursued through both practical and theoretical routes. In practice, the aim is to make machines capable of performing tasks which require intelligence as handled by a human. In theory, people want to pursue a scientific understanding of the computational principles underlying intelligent behavior, as manifested in humans and other animals. Both routes need to propose and understand operational principles of thought and action in computational terms. These principles may form the foundations of computer implementations of thought and action and, if suitably grounded in experimental method, may in some ways contribute to explanations of human thought and behavior.

AI research has been applied in broad ways. For instance, computer programs play chess at an expert level, assess insurance and credit risks, automatically identify objects from images, and search the contents of the Internet. From the scientific perspective, however, the aim of understanding intelligence from a computational point of view remains elusive. As an example, current programs for automatic reasoning can prove useful theorems concerning the correctness of large-scale digital circuitry, but exhibit little or no common sense. Current language-processing programs can translate simple sentences into database queries, but the programs are misled by the kind of idioms, metaphors, conversational ploys or ungrammatical expressions that we take for granted. Current vision programs can recognize a simple set of human faces in standard poses, but are misled by changes of illumination, or natural changes in facial expression and pose, or changes in cosmetics, spectacles or hairstyle. Current knowledge-based medical-expert systems can diagnose an infectious disease and prescribe an antibiotic therapy but, if you describe your motor car to the system, it will tell you what kind of meningitis your car has; the system does not know that cars do not get diseases. Current learning systems can forecast financial trends, given historical data, but cannot predict the date of Easter nor prime numbers given a large set of examples.

Inspired by the capacities of the human brain, AI-based models integrate the specific attributes of various disciplines, such as mathematics, physics, computer science and, recently, environmental engineering applications. AI-based prediction models have a significant potential for solving complex environmental applications that include large amounts of independent parameters and nonlinear relationships. Because of their predictive capabilities and nonlinear characteristics, several AI-based modeling techniques, such as artificial neural networks, fuzzy logic and adaptive neuro-fuzzy inference systems, have recently been conducted in the modeling of various real-life processes in the energy engineering field.

In this chapter, the basis of two widely used AI-based techniques, namely artificial neural networks and support vector machines, is theoretically summarized and important mathematical aspects of these methods are highlighted. Moreover, computational issues, and respective advantages of these methods are described.

3.2. Artificial neural networks

In the human brain, neurons are connected as a network to implement intelligent control and thinking. Inspired by this biological structure, an artificial neural network was proposed for supervised learning. The word "artificial" indicates it is a mathematical model, and it differs from a brain neural network. A typical neural network consists of an interconnected group of artificial neurons, and it contains information using a connection list approach to computation. Modern neural networks are nonlinear statistical data modeling tools. They are usually used to model complex relationships between inputs and outputs or to find patterns in data. Let us introduce this computational model, starting from the basic element and the simplest structure.

3.2.1. *Single-layer perceptron*

Figure 3.1(a) shows the basic computational element of a neural network which is often called a node or a neuron. It receives input I_i from some other units, or perhaps from an external source. Each input I_i has an associated weight w_i, which can be modified so as to train the model. Each neuron is composed of two units. The first unit adds products of weight coefficients and input signals. The second unit realizes the nonlinear function, called neuron activation function, i.e. $f(.)$. The output of this neuron is denoted by y:

$$y = f(\sum_i w_i I_i + bias) \qquad [3.1]$$

Its output y, in turn, can serve as an input to other units. The whole network consists of a topology graph of neurons, each of which computes an activation function of the inputs carried on the in-edges and sends the output on its out-edges. The inputs and outputs are weighed by weights w_{ij} and shifted by a *bias* factor specific to each neuron.

Figure 3.1(b) gives the simplest neural network example which contains a single output layer. Inputs are fed directly to the output via a series of weights, no other hidden neurons exist. This structure is called a single-layer perceptron.

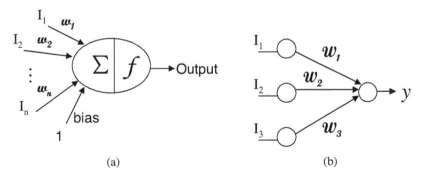

(a)   (b)

Figure 3.1. *Example of one neuron a) and a single-layer perceptron b)*

In this simple neural network, the sum of the products of the weights and inputs is calculated in each node, i.e. $\sum_i w_i I_i$. For example, if the value of the output is above a certain threshold t, the neuron takes the activated value, otherwise it takes the deactivated value. It can be formulated as follows:

$$y = \left\{ \begin{array}{ll} 1, & \text{if } \sum_i w_i I_i \geq t \\ -1, & \text{if } \sum_i w_i I_i < t \end{array} \right. \hspace{2cm} [3.2]$$

Neurons with this kind of activation function are also called artificial neurons or linear threshold units. In the literature, the term "perceptron" often refers to networks consisting of just one of these units. A perceptron can be created using any value for the activated and deactivated states as long as the threshold value lies between the two. Typically, the output of most perceptrons is either 1 or -1 with a threshold equal to 0.

Perceptrons can be trained by a simple learning algorithm that is usually called the delta rule. It calculates the errors between estimated output and sample output data, and uses this to create an adjustment to the weights, thus implementing a form of gradient descent. For a neuron j, with activation function $f(x)$, the delta rule for j's i^{th} weight w_{ji}, is given by:

$$\Delta w_{ji} = \alpha(t_j - y_j)f'(h_j)x_i \hspace{2cm} [3.3]$$

where α is a small constant called learning rate, $f(x)$ is the neuron's activation function, t_j is the jth target output, h_j is the summation of inputs $\sum x_i w_{ji}$, y_i is the actual output $y_i = f(h_j)$, x_i is the ith input.

It is very important to choose an appropriate activation function for each neuron. Usually, all neurons in a specific network share the same function. The common choices are:

– identity, i.e. $f(x) = x$;

– sigmoid, i.e. $f(x) = \frac{1}{1+e^{-x}}$, also known as logistic function;

– tanh, i.e. $f(x) = \frac{e^x - e^{-x}}{e^x + e^{-x}}$;

– step, i.e.

$$f(x) = \left\{ \begin{array}{ll} 1, & \text{if } x \geq 0 \\ -1, & \text{if } x < 0 \end{array} \right. .$$

Single-unit perceptrons are limited in performance. They are only capable of learning linearly separable patterns. For example, the simple, yet classic XOR function cannot be solved by a single-layer perceptron network since we cannot find a linear hyperplane to separate these two classes.

3.2.2. *Feed forward neural network*

The above single-layer perceptron is exactly a simple example of a feed forward neural network. In a feed forward network, the information transfers forward from input nodes, through hidden nodes (if any) to the output nodes, in only one direction. There are no cycles or loops in the network. The common feed forward network is a multi-layer perceptron (MLP) which contains one or more layers of hidden neurons, as shown in Figure 3.2. The neurons in the hidden layers are not directly accessible.

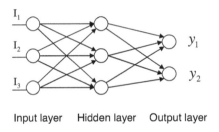

Input layer   Hidden layer   Output layer

Figure 3.2. *Feed forward neural network*

The training of an MLP is usually accomplished by using a back-propagation algorithm which involves two steps. Suppose that we have chosen the network's structure, activation function, and that free parameters for each node are initialized, then the forward step and the backward step are defined as follows:

– *forward step*: during this phase, the free parameters of the network, including weights and bias, are fixed, and the input signal is propagated through the network layer-by-layer. The output of the previous node is fed as input to the next node. The equation is the same as [3.1]. The forward phase finishes with the computation of an error signal $e_i = |t_i - y_i|$ where y_i is the estimated target in response to the input x_i and t_i is the actual sample target;

– *backward step*: the error signal e_i is propagated through the network in the backward direction, also layer-by-layer. It is during this phase that adjustments (see equation [3.3]) are applied to the free parameters of each neuron so as to minimize the squared estimation error.

There are two basic ways to implement back-propagation learning, namely the batch mode and the online mode:

– *batch mode*: in this mode, adjustments are made to the free parameters of the network on an epoch-by-epoch basis, where each epoch consists of the entire set of training examples. The batch mode is best suited for nonlinear regression;

– *online mode (or sequential mode)*: in this mode of back-propagation learning, adjustments are made to the free parameters of the network on an example-by-example basis. This mode is suited for pattern classification.

The advantage of a back-propagation learning algorithm is that it is simple to implement and computationally efficient due to the fact that its complexity is linear in the synaptic weights of the network. However, a major limitation of this algorithm is that the convergence is not always guaranteed and can be excruciatingly slow, particularly when the network topology is large.

There are many ways that feed forward neural networks can be constructed. Besides input and output layers, we must consider how many hidden layers we should have, and how many neurons in each layer. Using too few neurons in the hidden layers will result in under fitting which further leads to insufficient detection ability of the model on the signals in a complicated dataset. In contrast, using too many neurons in the hidden layers can result in several problems. First, it might cause an overfitting problem which leads to poor generalization ability on testing datasets. The second problem is the training time which will increase since the topology complexity is high. Neural networks with two hidden layers can represent functions with any kind of shape. Currently, there is no theoretical reason to use neural networks with more than two hidden layers for many practical problems. Some experiments are required to determine the optimal structure for the feed forward neural network. Readers can refer to [REE 99] for more details.

3.2.3. *Radial basis functions network*

Another popular layered feed forward network is the radial basis function (RBF) network. It has important properties of universal approximation. It is a paradigm of neural networks, which was developed considerably later than that of perceptrons. Like perceptrons, the RBF networks have a layered structure, which is composed of exactly three layers, i.e. only a single layer of hidden neurons. A simple example of this type of neural network is shown in Figure 3.3.

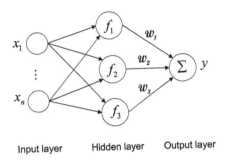

Input layer   Hidden layer   Output layer

Figure 3.3. *Simple radial basis functions neural network architecture*

For each layer, it has the following properties:

– *input layer*: there is only one neuron in the input layer for each predictor variable. In the case of categorical variables, $N - 1$ neurons are used where N represents the number of categories. The input neurons (or processing before the input layer) standardize the range of values by subtracting the median and dividing by the interquartile range. The input neurons then feed the values to each of the neurons in the hidden layer;

– *hidden layer*: this layer has a variable number of neurons (the optimal number is determined by the training process). Each neuron consists of a radial basis function centered on a point with as many dimensions as there are predictor variables. The activation function is given by:

$$f_j(x) = exp \left[\frac{-(X - \mu_j)^T}{\sum_j (X - \mu_j)} \right] \quad \text{for } j = 1, ..., L$$

where X is the input feature vector, L is the number of hidden neurons, μ_j and $\sum_j$ are the mean and the covariance matrix of the jth Gaussian function. The spread (radius) of the RBF function may be different for each dimension. The centers and spreads are determined by the training process. When presented with the x vector of input values from the input layer, a hidden neuron computes the Euclidean distance of the test case from the neuron's center point and then applies the RBF kernel function to this distance using the spread values. The resulting value is passed to the summation layer;

– *output layer*: the value coming out of a neuron in the hidden layer is multiplied by a weight associated with the neuron ($W_1, W_2, ..., W_n$ in this figure) and passed to the summation which adds up the weighted values and presents this sum as the output of the network, as follows:

$$y_k = \sum_{j=1}^{L} w_{jk} f_j(X)$$

In other words, the output neurons contain only the identity function. For classification problems, there is one output (and a separate set of weights and summation unit) for each target category. The value output for a category is the probability that the case being evaluated has that category.

RBF networks differ from multilayer perceptrons in the following fundamental respects. The former consists of local approximators, whereas the latter consists of global approximators. The former has a single hidden layer, whereas the latter can have any number of hidden layers. The output layer of an RBF network is always linear, whereas in a multilayer perceptron it can be either linear or nonlinear. The activation function of the hidden layer in an RBF network computes the Euclidean distance between the input signal vector and parameter vector of the network, whereas the activation function of a multilayer perceptron computes the inner product between the input signal vector and the pertinent synaptic weight vector.

When training RBF networks, the following parameters are determined:

– the number of neurons in the hidden layer;

– the coordinates of the center of each hidden-layer RBF function;

– the radius (spread) of each RBF function in each dimension;

– the weights applied to the RBF function outputs as they are passed to the summation layer.

RBF networks use memory-based learning for their design. Specifically, the summation on the output neuron means learning can be viewed as a curve-fitting problem in high-dimensional space.

A large variety of methods have been used to train RBF networks. One of them uses K-means clustering to find cluster centers which are then used as the centers for the RBF functions. However, K-means clustering is a computationally intensive procedure, and it often does not generate the optimal number of centers. Another common approach is to use a random subset of the training points as the centers.

3.2.4. *Recurrent neural network*

Recurrent neural networks (RNNs) differ in a fundamental way from feed forward architectures in the sense that they not only operate on an input space but also on an internal state space, a trace of what has already been processed by the network. Figure 3.4 shows a simple example where nodes s retain internal states, weights w_2 are recurrent weights. This additional layer is also called a "context" layer. At each time step, new inputs are fed into the RNN. The previous contents of the hidden layer are copied into the context layer. These are then fed back into the hidden layer in the next time step. The network recurrently influences itself by including the output in the following computation steps.

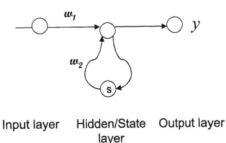

Input layer   Hidden/State   Output layer
layer

Figure 3.4. *Simple recurrent neural network*

There are various types of recurrent networks of nearly an arbitrary form. It is obvious that such a recurrent network is capable of computing more than the ordinary MLP. Indeed, if the recurrent weights are set to 0, the recurrent network will be reduced to an ordinary MLP. In addition, the recurrence generates different network-internal states so that different inputs can result in different outputs in the context of the network state.

For an arbitrary unit in a recurrent network, its activation at time t is defined as:

$$y_i(t) = f_i(net_i(t-1))$$

At each time step, activation propagates forward only through one layer of connections. Once a certain level of activation is present in the network, it will continue to flow around the units, even in the absence of any new input whatsoever. Now, the network can be represented by a time series of inputs, which requires that it produces an output based on this series. These networks can be used to model various novel kinds of problems. However, these networks also bring us many new difficult issues in training.

One way to meet these requirements is illustrated in the above network known as an Elman network, or as a simple recurrent network. Processing is done as follows:

– copy inputs for time t to the input units;

– compute hidden unit activations using net input from input units and from "context" layer;

– compute output unit activations as usual;

– copy new hidden unit activations to "context" layer.

For computing the activation, cycles have been eliminated, and therefore our requirement that the activations of all posterior nodes be known is met. In the same way, in computing errors, all trainable weights are fed forward only, so the standard back-propagation algorithm can be applied as before. The weights from the copy layer to the hidden layer play a special role in error computation. The error signal they receive comes from the hidden units, and therefore depends on the error at the hidden units at time step t. The activations in the hidden units, on the other hand, are just the activation of the hidden units at time $t-1$. Thus, in training, a gradient of an error function is considered, which is determined by the activations at the present and previous time steps.

A generalization of this approach is to copy the input and hidden unit activations for a number of previous time steps. The more context (in "context" layers) is maintained, the more history is explicitly included in the gradient computation. This approach is known as back propagation through time (BPTT). It can be seen as an approximation to the ideal of computing a gradient which takes into consideration not just the most recent inputs, but also all of the inputs seen so far by the network. This approach seeks to approximate the computation of a gradient based on all past inputs, while retaining the standard back-propagation algorithm. BPTT has been used in a number of applications. The main task is to produce a particular output sequence in response to specific input sequences. The downside of BPTT is that it requires a large amount of storage, computation and training examples in order to work well. To compute the true temporal gradient, we can use a method called real-time recurrent learning [WIL 94].

3.2.5. *Recursive deterministic perceptron*

The topology of recursive deterministic perceptron (RDP) feed forward neural network is dynamically increasing while learning. This special neural network model can solve any two-class classification problems and the convergence is always guaranteed [TAJ 98b]. It is a multilayer generalization of the single-layer perceptron topology and essentially retains the ability to deal with nonlinearly separable sets.

The construction of RDP does not require predefined parameters since they are automatically generated. The basic idea is to augment the dimension of the input vector by addition of intermediate neurons (INs), i.e. by incrementing affine dimension. These INs are added progressively at each time step, obtained by selecting a subset of points from the augmented input vectors. Selection of the subset is done so that it is linearly separable from the subset containing the rest of the augmented input points. Therefore, each new IN is obtained using linear separation methods. The algorithm stops when the two classes become linearly separable at a higher dimension. Hence, RDP neural network reports completely correct the decision boundary on the training dataset, and the knowledge extracted can be expressed as a finite union of open polytopes [TAJ 98a]. Some fundamental definitions of the RDP neural network are now discussed.

DEFINITION 3.1.– *An RDP on $\mathbb{R}^d$, denoted by P, is defined as a sequence $[(w_0, t_0), ..., (w_n, t_n)]$ such that $w_i \in \mathbb{R}^{d+i}$ and $t_i \in \mathbb{R}$, for $0 \leq i \leq n$, where*

- *for $0 \leq i \leq n$, (w_i, t_i) is termed an IN of P;*

- *height(P) is determined by the number of INs in P;*

- *$P(i, j)$ stands for the RDP $[(w_i, t_i), ..., (w_j, t_j)]$ and*

$$0 \leq i \leq j \leq height(P) - 1,$$

where $P(i, j)$ is on $\mathbb{R}^{d+i}$, and so $P = P(0, n)$.

DEFINITION 3.2.– *(Semantic of RDP). Let P be an RDP on $\mathbb{R}^d$. The function $\mathcal{F}(P)$ is defined in $\mathbb{R}^d$, such that:*

- *if $height(P) = 1$ then:*

$$\mathcal{F}(P)(x) = \begin{cases} -1, & \text{if } w^T x + t < 0 \\ 1, & \text{if } w^T x + t > 0 \end{cases};$$

- *if $height(P) > 1$ then:*

$$\mathcal{F}(P)(x) = \begin{cases} \mathcal{F}(P(1, n))(Adj(x, -1)), & \text{if } w_0^T x + t_0 < 0 \\ \mathcal{F}(P(1, n))(Adj(x, 1)), & \text{if } w_0^T x + t_0 > 0 \end{cases}$$

DEFINITION 3.3.– *Let X and Y be two subsets of $\mathbb{R}^d$ and let P be an RDP on $\mathbb{R}^d$. Then, X and Y are linearly separable by P if $(\forall x \in X, \mathcal{F}(P)(x) = c_1)$ and $(\forall y \in Y, \mathcal{F}(P)(y) = c_2)$ where $\{c_1, c_2\} = \{-1, 1\}$, and this is denoted by $X \parallel_P Y$.*

The last definition provides the criterion of termination of RDP training. Different choices of the linear separability testing method would influence the model convergence time and topology size. In [ELI 06] and [ELI 11], Elizondo *et al.* empirically studied six common choices, including simplex, convex hull, support vector machines (SVM), perceptron, Anderson and Fisher. In terms of convergence rate and topology size, the RDP with simplex outperforms all others. The RDP with SVM is comparable to RDP with simplex only in topology size. However, in terms of generalization ability, there is no apparent advantage for any method. Therefore, simplex is chosen as the linear separability testing method in our method when constructing a RDP neural network.

There are three logic sequences for constructing RDP neural networks: batch, incremental and modular [TAJ 98a]. The one adopted in our study is the incremental RDP since it will bring us the simplest topology. In this progressive learning, the network trains a single data point at a time. This is highly parallel to the physical reality since, as the operating conditions vary with time, the model adapts itself for fault identification. As learning proceeds, the network first tries to classify the data point within the existing framework. If the classification is not possible, the knowledge is interpolated by modifying the last IN or adding a new IN without disturbing the previously obtained knowledge. The training continues further until all the remaining points are classified by the network model. The procedure of this algorithm is shown in Figure 3.5.

3.2.6. *Applications of neural networks*

In machine learning and data mining, applications of neural networks are powerful tools in solving problems such as prediction, classification, change and deviation detection, knowledge discovery, response modeling and time series analysis. Since they have a large variety of forms and models, they have been successfully applied to a broad spectrum of data-intensive applications.

One of the popular applications is economic and financial analysis; in investment analysis, for instance to attempt to predict the movement of stocks currencies from previous data. There, they are replacing earlier simpler linear models. They are also applicable to decide whether an applicant for a loan is a good or bad credit risk. Rules for mortgage decisions are extracted from past decisions made by experienced evaluators, resulting in a network that has a high level of agreement with human experts. Other applications include credit rating, bankruptcy prediction, fraud detection, rating, price forecasts, etc.

In medical analysis, they are widely used to cardiopulmonary diagnostics. The way neural networks work in this area or other areas of medical diagnosis is by the comparison of many different models. A patient may have regular checkups in a particular area, increasing the possibility of detecting a disease or dysfunction. There is also some research using neural networks in the detection and evaluation of medical phenomena, treatment cost estimation, etc.

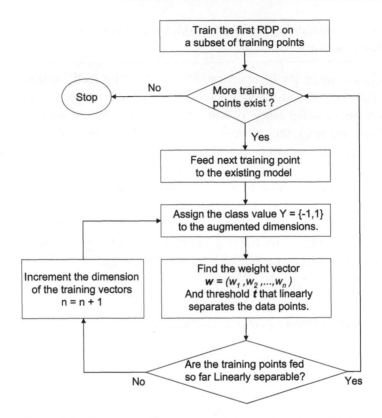

Figure 3.5. *Flowchart of the incremental recursive deterministic perceptron model training*

In industry, neural networks are used for process control, quality control, temperature and force prediction. They have been used to monitor the state of aircraft engines. By monitoring vibration levels and sound, an early warning of engine problems can be given. British Rail has also been testing a similar application for monitoring diesel engines.

In signature analysis, as a mechanism for comparing signatures made, e.g. in a bank, with those stored. This is one of the first large-scale applications of neural networks in US, and is also one of the first to use a neural network chip.

In some of the best speech recognition systems built so far, speech is first presented as a series of spectral slices to a recurrent network. Each output of the network represents the probability of a specific speech sound, e.g. /i/, /p/, etc, given both present and recent inputs. The probabilities are then interpreted by a hidden Markov model which tries to recognize the whole utterance.

In energy computation, neural networks are playing a significant role, mostly used on electrical load forecasting, energy demand forecasting, short- and long-term load estimation, predicting gas/coal index prices, power control systems and hydrodam monitoring.

Artificial neural networks (ANNs) are also widely used in other applications, such as image processing, sports betting, quantitative weather forecasting, optimization problems, routing, making horse and dog racing picks, agricultural production estimates, games development, etc.

3.3. Support vector machines

SVMs are a set of methods that extract models or patterns from data. They are usually thought to be the best supervised learning algorithms in solving problems such as classification, regression, transduction, novelty detection and semi-supervised learning. A basic idea of these algorithms is the structural risk minimization (SRM) inductive principle, which aims at minimizing the generalization error through minimizing a summation of empirical risk and a Vapnik Chervonenkis (VC) dimension term. In other words, it trades off the model performance in fitting the training data (minimize the empirical risk term) with the model complexity (minimize the VC dimension term) [VAP 95]. Therefore, this principle is different from the commonly used empirical risk minimization (ERM) principle which only minimizes the training error. Based on this principle, SVMs usually achieve a higher generalization performance in solving nonlinear problems than other supervised learning algorithms that only implement the ERM principle.

This section will introduce SVM algorithms. First, the principles of SVM for classification are introduced in section 3.3.1. Then, the crucial issue of this algorithm, quadratic problem (QP) solvers, is presented in section 3.3.7. Another algorithm for regression purpose is introduced in section 3.3.2. This algorithm will be used in later chapters. Other extensions of SVM, such as one-class SVM and transductive SVM, are then briefly introduced. Finally, some applications of SVMs are described in section 3.3.8 in order to show the high popularity of this model.

3.3.1. *Support vector classification*

SVM for classification, called support vector classification (SVC), aims at finding a hyperplane to separate two classes with maximum margin. Given training dataset X that includes l samples, let x_i denote the ith sample, y_i denote the corresponding label with the value either -1 or +1, $i = 1, 2, ..., l$. Let us start from a linearly separable classification problem. Figure 3.6 gives a simple example where each sample has only two dimensions. We use solid circles to represent the points whose label is '1' and use empty circles to denote the points with label '-1'. Our aim is to find the optimal hyperplane that can separate these two classes and then work well on the prediction of labels for unknown new points. We formulate this hyperplane (classifier) as follows.

$$h_{w,b}(x) = g(w^T x + b) \qquad\qquad [3.4]$$

where $g(z) = 1$ if $z \geq 0$, or $g(z) = -1$ if $z < 0$, so that in Figure 3.6 the best separating line is defined by $w^T + b = 0$. Then the training problem becomes how to find the best separating line. This means how to find the optimal values for parameters w and b.

Intuitively, if one point is far from the decision boundary, we may have more confidence in labelling it with '1' or '-1'. So, we know that the best separating line is the one which has the largest distance from the points in both sides. Thus, the largest distance is called the maximum margin. Based on this consideration, we can derive the following optimization problem for finding w and b.

$$\min_{w,b} \quad \frac{1}{2}||w||^2$$

under the constraint $\quad y_i(w^T x_i + b) \geq 1, \quad i = 1, ..., l$

This is a convex quadratic optimization problem (QP) with linear constraints and it can be efficiently solved by off-the-shelf quadratic problem solvers.

However, in practice, most of the problems are not linearly separable, which means that the above ideal case does not always happen. To make the classifier suitable for nonlinearly separable samples, we add the l_1-regularization to the function:

$$\min_{w,b} \quad \frac{1}{2}||w||^2 + C\sum_{i=1}^{l}\xi_i \qquad\qquad [3.5]$$

under the constraint $\quad y_i(w^T x_i + b) \geq 1 - \xi_i, \quad i = 1,...,l \qquad [3.6]$

$$\xi_i \geq 0, \quad i = 1,...,l \qquad\qquad [3.7]$$

where ξ_i is an added slack variable corresponding to sample i. By doing this, the classifier will allow outliers which are misclassified, i.e. $\xi_i > 0$. In other words, the optimal hyperplane becomes less sensitive to the outliers. C is a user-defined constant value which is used to control the sensitivity to outliers, i.e. if C is large, the classifier is more sensitive to the outliers. By adding the regularization term, the problem is becoming more complicated and cannot be easily solved directly.

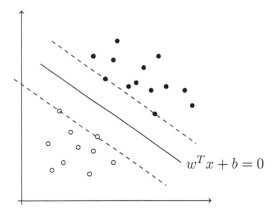

Figure 3.6. *Linearly separable classification problem*

Let us use the method based on Lagrange multipliers to derive the dual form of this optimization problem. The dual form is a finite optimization problem. One advantage of the dual form is that we can use kernel tricks to allow the model to solve nonlinear problems. By introducing Lagrangian multipliers, we can form the Lagrangian as:

$$L(w, b, \xi, \alpha, r) = \frac{1}{2} w^T w + C \sum_{i=1}^{l} \xi_i - \sum_{i=1}^{l} \alpha_i [y_i (w^T x_i + b)$$

$$-1 + \xi_i] - \sum_{i=1}^{l} r_i \xi_i$$

where α and r are the Lagrange multipliers with the constraints $\alpha_i, r_i \geq 0$. Taking the partial derivative of this Lagrangian with respect to w to be equal to zero, leads to:

$$\Delta_w L = w - \sum_{i=1}^{l} \alpha_i y_i x_i = 0 \qquad [3.8]$$

which summarizes to:

$$w = \sum_{i=1}^{l} \alpha_i y_i x_i \qquad [3.9]$$

Similarly, taking the partial derivatives with respect to b and ξ to be zero, we then obtain:

$$\sum_{i=1}^{l} \alpha_i y_i = 0 \qquad [3.10]$$

$$C - \alpha_i y_i - r_i = 0 \qquad [3.11]$$

Inserting equation [3.9] back to the Lagrangian, and using equations [3.10], and [3.11], we obtain after simplification the dual form of this problem:

$$\max_{\alpha} \sum_{i=1}^{l} \alpha_i - \frac{1}{2} \sum_{i,j=1}^{l} y_i y_j \alpha_i \alpha_j < x_i, x_j > \qquad [3.12]$$

under the constraint $0 \leq \alpha_i \leq C, \quad i = 1, ..., l \qquad [3.13]$

$$\sum_{i=1}^{l} \alpha_i y_i = 0, \quad i = 1, ..., l \qquad [3.14]$$

where α is a vector of l variables which need to be optimized. So, this problem is a convex quadratic optimization problem with linear constraints. From equation [3.9], if we find out α by solving this dual problem, we can write the decision function as:

$$w^T x + b = (\sum_{i-1}^{l} \alpha_i y_i x_i)^T x + b \qquad [3.15]$$

$$= \sum_{i=1}^{l} \alpha_i y_i < x_i, x > + b \qquad [3.16]$$

At this point, it is important to note that this form is sparse since there are many α_i's equal to zero.

The dual form of the SVM can be written in the following convex quadratic form:

$$\min_{\alpha} \quad \frac{1}{2} \alpha^T Q \alpha - \sum_{i=1}^{l} \alpha_i \qquad [3.17]$$

under the constraint $y^T \alpha = 0$ \qquad [3.18]

$$0 \leq \alpha_i \leq C \quad \forall i = 1, 2, ..., l \qquad [3.19]$$

where Q is a l by l positive semi-definite matrix. Each element of Q has the form $Q_{ij} = y_i y_j < x_i, x_j >$. We see that the entire algorithm is written in terms of the dot product $< x_i, x_j >$. If we use $\phi(x)$ to substitute x, then the dot product $< x_i, x_j >$ can be replaced by $< \phi(x_i), \phi(x_j) >$, and we see there is no change to the algorithm. But, the important thing is that $\phi(x)$ could be a mapping from a lower dimensional space to a higher feature space. So that for some problems of which points are nonlinearly separable in the lower dimensional space, as long as we map them into higher dimensional space, it is possible to find a linear hyperplane for the newly generated points in the new feature space. This means we are able to solve nonlinear problems by this mapping technique. To make this algorithm more practical, we need to introduce the kernel functions.

Suppose that we have the feature mapping ϕ, we define the kernel function as $K(x, z) = \phi(x)^T \phi(z)$, then everywhere the inner product $< \phi(x_i), \phi(x_j) >$ can be further replaced by the kernel function $K(x_i, x_j)$.

The elements of the matrix Q now become $Q_{ij} = y_i y_j K(x_i, x_j)$, hence, Q is also called a kernel matrix. This replacement demonstrates that there is no need to explicitly express the form of the mapping ϕ. However, what kind of function can be used as the kernel function? Intuitively, we know that a valid kernel should correspond to some feature mapping. In fact, the necessary and sufficient condition for a function to be a valid kernel is the following Mercer condition. Hence, the valid kernel is also called a Mercer kernel.

THEOREM 3.1.– Given $K : \mathbb{R}^n \times \mathbb{R}^n \mapsto \mathbb{R}$, for K to be a valid kernel, it is necessary and sufficient that for any given training set $\{x_1, x_2, ..., x_l\}, l < \infty$, the corresponding kernel matrix Q is symmetric positive semi-definite.

Only a Mercer kernel can be expressed in an equal form to $< \phi(x_i), \phi(x_j) >$. In practice, the commonly used kernel functions are:

– linear function, i.e. $K(x, z) = x^T z$;

– polynomial function, i.e. $K(x, z) = (\gamma x^T z + coef)^d$;

– radial basis function (RBF), i.e. $K(x, z) = exp(-\gamma|x - z|^2)$;

– sigmoid function, i.e. $K(x, z) = \tanh(\gamma x^T z + coef)$.

Here, we use x and z to substitute two samples x_i and x_j, respectively.

The idea of kernels broadens the applicability of the SVMs, allowing the algorithm to work efficiently in the high-dimensional feature space. This kernel formulation not only works well for SVMs, but also works for any learning algorithm which can be written in terms of inner product [SCH 02].

Since we have developed the kernel function K, if the problem is a classification problem of which the label of an instance is '−1' or '1', we can use the following decision function to predict the labels of the new input x:

$$sgn \left(\sum_{i=1}^{l} \alpha_i y_i K(x_i, x) + b \right) \qquad [3.20]$$

where b is a constant value which can be easily calculated in the training step, and

$$sgn(x) = \left\{ \begin{array}{ll} -1, & \text{for } x < 0 \\ 1, & \text{for } x > 0 \end{array} \right. \qquad [3.21]$$

3.3.2. ε-support vector regression

Section 3.3.1 has discussed SVM for classification use, while in practice, there are many requirements for regression problems of which the target is a real continuous variable. For instance, the hourly energy consumption of a building is real continuous, it cannot be solved by the classification model. Support vector regression (SVR) is designed for this purpose [DRU 96]. In this section, we introduce its principles. To make the estimation robust and sparse, we use an ε-insensitive loss function in constructing the model.

$$L(y - f(x)) = \left\{ \begin{array}{ll} 0 & \text{if } |y - f(x)| \leq \varepsilon \\ |y - f(x)| - \varepsilon & \text{otherwise} \end{array} \right.$$

This loss function indicates an ε-tube around the predicted target values as shown in Figure 3.7.

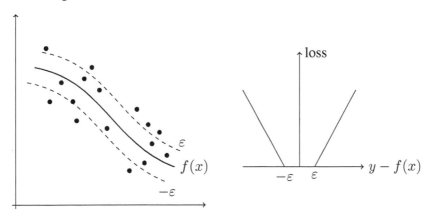

Figure 3.7. ε-tube for support vector regression

This means that we assume there is no deviation of the predicted values from the measured ones if they lie inside the tube (within the threshold ε). It is for the same reason that we introduce a slack variable into SVC as described in section 3.3.1. Unlike SVC, where only one slack variable is involved, for SVR, we introduce two slack variables ξ_i and ξ_i^*, $i = 1, 2, ..., l$. The objective function is as follows.

$$\min \quad \frac{1}{2}\|w\|^2 + C(\sum_{i=1}^{l} \xi_i^* + \sum_{i=1}^{l} \xi_i) \qquad [3.22]$$

under the constraints

$$y_i - f(x_i) \leq \varepsilon + \xi_i^*$$

$$f(x_i) - y_i \leq \varepsilon + \xi_i$$

$$\xi_i^* \geq 0, \quad , \xi_i \geq 0, \qquad \qquad i = 1, 2, ..., l$$

where C is a regularizing constant, which determines the trade off between the capacity of $f(x)$ and the number of points outside the ε-tube. To find the saddle point of the function defined in equation [3.22] under the previous inequalities constraints, we can turn to the Lagrange function by introducing four Lagrange multipliers, α^*, α, γ^*, γ. The Lagrangian becomes:

$$L(w, b, \xi^*, \xi, \alpha^*, \alpha, \gamma^*, \gamma) = \frac{1}{2}\|w\|^2$$

$$+ C(\sum_{i=1}^{l} \xi_i^* + \sum_{i=1}^{l} \xi_i)$$

$$- \sum_{i=1}^{l} \alpha_i[y_i - (wx_i) - b + \varepsilon + \xi_i] - \alpha_i^*[y_i - (wx_i)$$

$$- b + \varepsilon + \xi_i^*]$$

$$- \sum_{i=1}^{l} l(\gamma_i^* \xi_i^* + \gamma\xi) \qquad [3.23]$$

The four Lagrange multipliers satisfied the constraints $\alpha^* \geq 0, \alpha \geq 0, \gamma^* \geq 0$ and $\gamma \geq 0, i = 1, 2, ..., l$. If the four relations

$$\frac{\partial L}{\partial w} = \frac{\partial L}{\partial b} = \frac{\partial L}{\partial \xi^*} = \frac{\partial L}{\partial \xi} = 0$$

occur, we are able to derive the following conditions,

$$w = \sum_{i=1}^{l} (\alpha_i^* - \alpha_i) x_i \qquad\qquad [3.24]$$

$$\sum_{i=1}^{l} \alpha_i^* = \sum_{i=1}^{l} \alpha_i \qquad\qquad [3.25]$$

$$0 \leq \alpha_i^* \leq C, \quad 0 \leq \alpha_i \leq C \qquad\qquad [3.26]$$

$$C = \alpha_i^* + \gamma_i^* = \alpha_i + \gamma_i, \qquad i = 1, 2, ..., l \qquad\qquad [3.27]$$

Inserting these conditions into the above Lagrangian, we obtain the solution of the optimization problem which is equal to the maximum of the function defined [3.23] with respect to the Lagrange multipliers. The next step is to find α_i^* and α_i in order to maximize the following function:

$$W(\alpha_i^*, \alpha_i) = \sum_{i=1}^{l} y_i(\alpha_i^* - \alpha_i) - \varepsilon \sum_{i=1}^{l} (\alpha_i^* + \alpha_i)$$

$$-\frac{1}{2} \sum_{i,j=1}^{l} (\alpha_i^* - \alpha_i)(\alpha_j^* - \alpha_j)(x_i \cdot x_j) \qquad\qquad [3.28]$$

under constraints [3.25] and [3.26], where $(x_i \cdot x_j)$ stands for the dot product of two vectors x_i and x_j. Normally, only a certain part of the samples satisfies the property of $\alpha_i^* - \alpha_i \neq 0$, which are called support vectors (SVs). In fact, only these samples lying outside the ε-tube will contribute to determining the objective function. As in SVC, it is possible to use kernel function $K(x_i \cdot y_i)$

to replace the dot product. Since we have w as in equation [3.24], the decision function can be developed to:

$$f(x) = \sum_{i=1}^{l} (\alpha_i^* - \alpha_i) K(x_i, x) + b \qquad [3.29]$$

where α_i^* and α_i are determined by maximizing the quadratic function defined in equation [3.28] under constraints [3.25] and [3.26].

3.3.3. *One-class support vector machines*

In some classification problems, the classes are not very clear and we are not able to clearly label the samples as two classes or multiple classes. Sometimes, only the positive class is known and the negative samples can belong to any distributions. It can be regarded as a $(1 + x)$-class problem. For instance, suppose we want to build a classifier which identifies researchers' web pages. While obtaining the training data, we can collect the positive samples by browsing some researchers' personal pages and form the negative samples which are not "a researcher's web page". Obviously, the negative samples vary in a large number of types and do not belong to any class. Therefore, it is hard to define the distribution of the negatives. In other words, "each negative sample is negative in its own way". This kind of problem cannot be formulated as a binary class classification problem.

We are mainly interested in the positive class and do not care too much about the negatives. One-class SVMs offer a solution to such classification problems [SCH 01]. The idea is to build a hypersphere which clusters the positive samples and separates them from the rest. Consider again the "maximum margin" and "soft margin" spirits, the hypersphere gives a boundary to most of the positive points, not all, to avoid overfitting. Suppose c is the center of the positive points, $\Phi(x)$ is the feature map, ξ is the slack variable, the one-class SVMs consist of solving the following problem:

$$\min_{R \in \mathbb{R}, \xi \in \mathbb{R}^l} \quad R^2 + \frac{1}{\nu l} \sum_i \xi_i$$

$$\text{under the constraint} \quad ||\Phi(x_i) - c||^2 \leq R^2 + \xi_i$$

$$\xi_i \geq 0, \quad i = 1, 2, ..., l$$

From this primal form, we can derive the dual form as:

$$\min_{\alpha} \quad \sum_{ij} \alpha_i \alpha_j K(x_i, x_j) - \sum_i \alpha_i K(x_i, x_i)$$

$$\text{under the constraints} \quad 0 \leq \alpha_i \leq \frac{1}{\nu l}$$

$$\sum_i \alpha_i = 1$$

where K is a kernel function and ν is an upper bound on the fraction of outliers which are outside the estimated region and a lower bound on the fraction of support vectors. The decision function is formulated as follows:

$$f(x) = sgn \left(R^2 - \sum_{ij} \alpha_i \alpha_j K(x_i, x_j) + 2 \sum_i \alpha_i K(x_i, x) - K(x, x) \right).$$

where $sgn(x)$ is defined in equation [3.21].

3.3.4. *Multiclass support vector machines*

When there are more than two classes in the data, and the aim is to build a classifier that can classify all of the classes, we call such problems multiclass classification problems. Multiclass SVMs are used to solve these problems. There are several approaches for implementing multiclass SVMs.

The first is a one-against-all method. The idea is straightforward and can be summarized as follows. Suppose there are k classes in the training data, we train one SVM for one-class, we suppose the samples in this class are positive and the rest from all other classes are negative. Therefore, we totally train k SVMs. Given a new sample, we assign it to the class with the highest objective value [VAP 98].

The second one is pairwise method. We construct a normal two-class SVM for each pair of classes. While training this SVM, we just use the training data within these two classes and ignore other training samples, so that, if there are k classes, we will train $k(k-1)/2$ SVMs. In the estimation, we use a voting strategy, i.e. given an unknown objective sample, we use each SVM to evaluate which class it belongs to, and the final decision is the class which gets the maximum votes. This method is first used in [FRI 96] and [KRE 99].

The third one is called pairwise coupling. This method is designed for the case where the output of the two-class SVM can be written as the posterior probability of the positive class. For a given unknown example, the selected posterior probabilities $p_i = Prob(\omega_i|x)$ are calculated as a combination of the probabilistic outputs of all binary classifiers. Then, the example is assigned to the class with the highest p_i. This method is proposed by Hastie and Tibshirani in [HAS 98]. However, the decision of an SVM is not a probabilistic value. Platt [PLA 99b] proposed a sigmoid function to map the decision of an SVM classifier to the positive class posterior probability:

$$Prob(\omega|x) = \frac{1}{1 + e^{Af+B}}$$

where A and B are the parameters and f is the decision of SVM with regard to sample x. Another model kernel logistic regression (KLR) [ROT 01] has the output form in terms of positive class posterior probability, so that it can be used directly as the binary classification in the pairwise coupling method [DUA 03].

3.3.5. v-*support vector machines*

When we stated one-class SVM in section 3.3.3, we introduced a new parameter v. We stated that it controls training errors and the number of support vectors. By introducing this parameter, Schölkopf *et al.* [SCH 00] have derived an SVM model for classification problems named v-SVC where the original parameter C is replaced by v. And also, for regression problems, the corresponding v-SVR is developed.

The primal form of v-SVC is defined by:

$$\min_{w,b,\xi,\rho} \frac{1}{2}||w||^2 - v\rho + \frac{1}{l}\sum_i \xi_i$$

under the constraints $y_i(w^T x_i + b) \geq \rho - \xi_i,$

$$\xi_i \geq 0, i = 1, 2, ..., l, \rho \geq 0.$$

We can derive the dual form as:

$$\min_{\alpha} \quad \frac{1}{2}\alpha^T Q\alpha$$

under the constraints $\quad 0 \leq \alpha_i \leq \frac{1}{l}, i = 1, ..., l$

$$e^T\alpha \geq \nu, \quad y^T\alpha = 0.$$

where Q is the kernel matrix. In ν-SVR, the new parameter is used to replace ε instead of C. The primal form can be written as:

$$\min_{w,b,\xi,\xi^*,\varepsilon} \quad \frac{1}{2}||w||^2 + C(\nu\varepsilon + \frac{1}{l}\sum_i(\xi_i + \xi_i^*))$$

under the constraints $\quad (w^T x_i + b) - z_i \leq \varepsilon + \xi_i,$

$$z_i - (w^T x_i + b) \leq \varepsilon + \xi_i^*,$$

$$\xi_i, \xi_i^* \geq 0, i = 1, ..., l, \varepsilon \geq 0.$$

The dual form becomes:

$$\min_{\alpha,\alpha^*} \quad \frac{1}{2}(\alpha - \alpha^*)^T Q(\alpha - \alpha^*) + z^T(\alpha - \alpha^*)$$

under the constraint $\quad \sum_i \alpha_i - \sum_i \alpha_i^* = 0,$

$$\sum_i \alpha_i + \sum_i \alpha_i^* \leq C\nu,$$

$$0 \leq \alpha, \alpha^* \leq C/l, \quad i = 1, ..., l.$$

The decision functions of ν-SVC and ν-SVR for a given new unlabeled sample x are the same as that of SVC and ε-SVR, which are given in equations [3.20] and [3.29] respectively.

3.3.6. *Transductive support vector machines*

The above introduced SVMs are trained on labeled training data and then used to predict the labels on unlabeled testing data. We can call these models inductive SVMs. Contrary to this idea, transductive SVM is trained on the combination of the labeled training data and unlabeled testing data. Therefore, it is a semi-supervised learning algorithm. The basic idea of transductive SVM is to build a hyperplane that maximizes the separation between labeled and unlabeled datasets [VAP 98].

Suppose there are l labeled data $\{(x_1, y_1), ..., (x_l, y_l)\}$ and u unlabeled data $\{x_1^*, ..., x_u^*\}$. To derive the hyperplane that separates these two datasets with maximum margin, first we label the unlabeled data by using an inductive SVM, suppose the resulting transductive data become $(x_1^*, y_1^*), ..., (x_u^*, y_u^*)$, then we solve the following problem:

$$\min_{w,b,\xi,\xi^*} \quad \frac{1}{2}||w||^2 + C\sum_{i=1}^{l}\xi_i + C^*\sum_{j=1}^{d}\xi_j^*$$

under the constraints $\quad y_i(w^T x_i + b) \geq 1 - \xi_i$

$$y_j^*(w^T x_j^* + b) \geq 1 - \xi_j^*$$

$$\xi_i \geq 0, \ i = 1, ..., l, \xi_j^* \geq 0, \ j = 1, ..., d.$$

where ξ and ξ^* are the slack variables and C and C^* are the two penalty constants. It is not necessary to use all of the unlabeled samples for learning, so that d $(d \leq u)$ is introduced to control the number of transductive samples. The dual form is:

$$\min_{\alpha,\alpha^*} \quad \sum_{i=1}^{n}\alpha_i + \sum_{j=1}^{d}\alpha_j^* - \frac{1}{2}\left(\sum_{i=1}^{n}\sum_{j=1}^{n}G(\alpha_i, \alpha_j) + 2\sum_{i=1}^{n}\sum_{j=1}^{d}G(\alpha_i, \alpha_j^*)\right.$$

$$\left. + \sum_{i=1}^{d}\sum_{j=1}^{d}G(\alpha_i^*, \alpha_j^*)\right)$$

under the constraints $\quad 0 \leq \alpha_i \leq C, \ 1 \leq i \leq n$

$$0 \leq \alpha_j^* \leq C, \ 1 \leq j \leq d$$

$$\sum_{i=1}^{n}y_i\alpha_i + \sum_{j=1}^{d}y_j^*\alpha_j^* = 0$$

where

$$G(\alpha_i, \alpha_j) = \alpha_i \alpha_j y_i y_j K(x_i, x_j),$$
$$G(\alpha_i, \alpha_j^*) = \alpha_i \alpha_j^* y_i y_j^* K(x_i, x_j^*),$$
$$G(\alpha_i^*, \alpha_j^*) = \alpha_i^* \alpha_j^* y_i^* y_j^* K(x_i^*, x_j^*).$$

The decision function is as follows:

$$f(x) = sgn\left(\sum_{i=1}^{n} \alpha_i y_i K(x_i, x) + \sum_{j=1}^{d} \alpha_j^* y_j^* K(x_j^*, x) + b \right)$$

where the function $sgn(x)$ is defined in equation [3.21].

3.3.7. *Quadratic problem solvers*

Let us first introduce the Karush–Kuhn–Tucher (KKT) conditions which determine whether or not the optimized variables are solutions to the primal and dual problems.

Since SVMs have several variations and their forms are complex, to avoid tedious notations, we use a general and simplified problem to discuss the optimality conditions. Consider the following convex optimization problem with an equality and an inequality constraint:

$$\min_{x} \quad f(x)$$

under the constraints $\quad g_i(x) \leq 0 \quad i = 1, ..., m$
$$h_j(x) = 0 \quad j = 1, ..., p$$

where $f(x)$ and $g(x)$ are the convex functions. The corresponding Lagrangian is

$$L(x, \alpha, \beta) = f(x) + \alpha^T g(x) + \beta^T h(x)$$

where $\alpha \in \mathbb{R}^m$ ($\alpha_i \geq 0$) and $\beta \in \mathbb{R}^p$ are the two vectors of Lagrange multipliers. The variables of the vector $x \in \mathbb{R}^n$ are called primal variables and

α_i's and β_i's are called dual variables. The optimization problem is equal to the following problems:

Primal problem: $\min\limits_{x}[\max\limits_{\alpha,\beta:\alpha_i\geq0,\forall i} L(x,\alpha,\beta)]$

Dual problem: $\max\limits_{\alpha,\beta:\alpha_i\geq0,\forall i}[\min\limits_{x} L(x,\alpha,\beta)]$

Suppose x^*, α, β (local minimum point), a solution of the optimization problem and satisfying the constraints, then there is a vector of α and a vector of β which satisfy the KKT conditions which are as follows:

$$\Delta f(x^*) + \alpha^T \Delta g(x^*) + \beta^T \Delta h(x^*) = 0 \qquad [3.30]$$

$$g_i(x^*) \leq 0, \quad i = 1,...,m \qquad [3.31]$$

$$h_j(x^*) = 0, \quad j = 1,...,p \qquad [3.32]$$

$$\alpha_i \geq 0, \quad i = 1,...,m \qquad [3.33]$$

$$\alpha_i g_i(x^*) = 0, \quad i = 1,...,m \qquad [3.34]$$

The first equation [3.30] is the gradient of the Lagrangian function, which indicates that the solution is the stationarity point of the Lagrangian function. Equations [3.31] and [3.32] guarantee that a solution is primal feasible, while equation [3.33] ensures that a solution is dual feasible. The latter is called the KKT dual complementarity condition which implies that if $\alpha_i > 0$ then $g_i(x^*) = 0$, in this case, we call the equality constraints active constraints. In SVM, the active constraints are support vectors. When the KKT conditions are fulfilled to the dual form of SVM, the following KKT dual complementarity condition can be derived:

$$\alpha_i = 0 \Rightarrow y_i(w^T x_i + b) \geq 1$$

$$\alpha_i = C \Rightarrow y_i(w^T x_i + b) \leq 1$$

$$0 < \alpha_i < C \Rightarrow y_i(w^T x_i + b) = 1$$

Many off-the-shelf quadratic problem solvers can be used to train SVMs. There are three important and widely considered methods, interior point, gradient descent and decomposition method. We will introduce the first two methods in the following two sections and leave the third to be stated in Chapter 6.

3.3.7.1. *Interior point method*

The idea behind the primal-dual interior point method is to solve the problem in terms of primal and dual forms simultaneously. The optimal solution point is found by searching and testing interior points in the feasible region iteratively. In thissection, we present the fundamentals of this algorithm as introduced in [MEH 92, WRI 97] and [SCH 02]. Let us consider the following convex quadratic problem which is a general dual form of SVMs:

$$\min_{\alpha} \quad \frac{1}{2}\alpha^T Q \alpha + c^T \alpha \qquad\qquad [3.35]$$

under the constraints $A\alpha = b$

$$l \leq \alpha \leq u$$

where $\alpha \in \mathbb{R}^n$ is a vector of free variables, $c \in \mathbb{R}^n$, $l \in \mathbb{R}^n$, $u \in \mathbb{R}^n$, $b \in \mathbb{R}^m$ are the vectors with constant value, $A \in \mathbb{R}^{m \times n}$ is a full rank coefficient matrix. To develop the dual form of this problem, we first change the inequalities constraint into positivity constraints by introducing two slack variables s and t, then the constraints become:

$$A\alpha = b \qquad\qquad [3.36]$$

$$\alpha - s = l \qquad\qquad [3.37]$$

$$\alpha + t = u \qquad\qquad [3.38]$$

$$s \geq 0 \qquad\qquad [3.39]$$

$$t \geq 0 \qquad\qquad [3.40]$$

Now, we will develop the dual form. By introducing five Lagrange multipliers $\lambda, k, -w, y, z$ to associate with the five constraints, respectively, then formulating the Lagrangian function $L(\alpha, \lambda, k, w, y, z)$ and letting

$$\frac{\partial L}{\partial \alpha} = 0, \frac{\partial L}{\partial s} = 0, \frac{\partial L}{\partial t} = 0,$$

we obtain the following equations:

$$Q\alpha + c - A^T \lambda - k + w = 0$$

$$y = k$$

$$z = w$$

We substitute these equations to the following problem which defines the dual form:

$$\max \quad L(\alpha, \lambda, k, w, y, z)$$

$$\text{under the constraints} \quad L'_\alpha = 0$$

$$y \geq 0$$

$$z \geq 0$$

and then we can develop the dual form of our problem defined in equation [3.35] as:

$$\max \quad -\frac{1}{2}\alpha^T Q\alpha + b^T\lambda + l^T k - u^T w \qquad [3.41]$$

$$\text{under the constraint} \quad Q\alpha + c - A^T\lambda + w = k \qquad [3.42]$$

$$k \geq 0 \qquad [3.43]$$

$$w \geq 0 \qquad [3.44]$$

where λ is the vector of dual variables. The KKT conditions are the constraints of the primal and dual forms [3.36]–[3.40] and [3.42]–[3.44] in addition with the complementarity conditions:

$$s_i k_i = 0, \quad t_i w_i = 0, \quad \forall i = 1, 2, ..., n \qquad [3.45]$$

These conditions mean that the duality gap is zero, which is equivalent to the fact that the primal and dual objective functions reach the equal extreme value. It is known that the KKT conditions provide the necessary and sufficient conditions for a solution to be optimal.

In the interior point algorithm, if a solution satisfies the primal and dual constraints, we say this solution is primal and dual feasible. We approach the optimal solution by trying candidate points in the feasible region step-by-step. The complementarity conditions [3.45] are used to determine the quality of the current solution. For this purpose, we do not try to find the solution for equation [3.45] directly, instead, we set the duality gap as μ (> 0) and decrease μ iteratively until the duality gap is small enough. Correspondingly, the complementarity conditions are modified as follows:

$$s_i k_i = \mu, \quad t_i w_i = \mu, \quad \forall i = 1, 2, ..., n \qquad [3.46]$$

In other words, we approximate the optimal solution (where the duality gap is zero) by an iterative predictor-corrector approach. At each iteration, for a given μ, we find a more feasible solution, then decrease μ and repeat until μ falls below a predefined tolerance, so that the substantial problem of interior point algorithm is how we move from the current point $(\alpha, \lambda, k, w, y, z)$ to the next point $(\alpha', \lambda', k', w', y', z')$. Let $(\Delta\alpha, \Delta\lambda, \Delta k, \Delta w, \Delta y, \Delta z)$ be the search direction, then the update occurs as:

$$(\alpha', \lambda', k', w', y', z') = (\alpha, \lambda, k, w, y, z) + (\Delta\alpha, \Delta\lambda, \Delta k, \Delta w, \Delta y, \Delta z)$$

Substitution into the KKT conditions, implies that the following conditions must be satisfied:

$$A(\alpha + \Delta\alpha) = b$$

$$\alpha + \Delta\alpha - s - \Delta s = l$$

$$\alpha + \Delta\alpha + t + \Delta t = u$$

$$Q(\alpha + \Delta\alpha) + c - A^T(\lambda + \Delta\lambda) + w + \Delta w = k + \Delta k$$

$$(s + \Delta s)(k + \Delta k) = \mu$$

$$(t + \Delta t)(w + \Delta w) = \mu$$

Suppose μ is given, then the Newton method is used to solve these equations. The augmentation of the free variables at each iteration can be derived as:

$$\begin{bmatrix} -H & A^T \\ A & 0 \end{bmatrix} \begin{bmatrix} \Delta\alpha \\ \Delta\lambda \end{bmatrix} \begin{bmatrix} \bar{r} \\ \bar{v} \end{bmatrix}$$

where

$$H = (Q + s^{-1}k + t^{-1}w),$$

and $\bar{r}$ and $\bar{v}$ are appropriately defined residues. Readers may consult [WRI 97] for more details. For solving $\Delta\lambda$, first we need to calculate the coefficient matrix $(AH^{-1}A^T)$. The calculation and factorization of this matrix is the most time-consuming process of the interior point method, leading to a computational cost in $O(n^3)$ and a memory requirement in $O(n^2)$ for each iteration. If Q is easily invertible, the algorithm would be more efficient.

3.3.7.2. *Stochastic gradient descent*

Gradient descent methods approximate the minimum of the objective by iteratively updating the variables in the direction of gradient descent. Two main steps are repeated in the algorithm, one is calculating the descent direction $P(\Delta f(w))$ which is some function of the gradient and searching for step size η ($\eta > 0$, also called learning rate), the other one is updating the variables in w.

- *Step 1*: calculating the direction $P(\Delta f(w^t))$ and step size η_t;
- *Step 2*: updating variables $w^{t+1} = w^t - \eta_t P(\Delta f(w^t))$.

These methods are common solvers for convex optimization problems. However, a well-known disadvantage is the slow convergence rate, and even under some circumstances, the convergence may not be guaranteed. By considering this problem, Zhang [ZHA 04] introduced the stochastic gradient descent method in solving large-scale linear prediction problems. This method can easily be applied for SVM QP optimization, performing directly on the primal form. Different from batch gradient descent methods, in which the whole data samples are examined in each iteration, Zhang's stochastic gradient descent method requires only one random sample from the training data in each iteration. The algorithm is guaranteed to be convergent in a finite number of iterations. As described in [ZHA 04], the number of iterations T satisfies $1/T = O(\epsilon^2)$ where ϵ is a predefined accuracy.

When this algorithm is used for the SVM QP solver, it works as follows. Suppose that (x, y) is one sample of the training set A, the size of A is m, the loss function is $l(w, x, y)$, then the objective function can be written as:

$$f(w) = \frac{\lambda}{2}||w||^2 + \frac{1}{m} \sum_{(x,y) \in A} l(w, x, y)$$ [3.47]

In iteration t, suppose that the sample (x_t, y_t) is chosen, then we form the descent direction as:

$$S_t^{-1}(\lambda w_{t-1} + l'_w(w_{t-1}, x_t, y_t))$$

where S is a preconditioner used to accelerate the convergence rate. Therefore, the variables are updated by the relation:

$$w_t = w_{t-1} - \eta_t S_t^{-1}(\lambda w_{t-1} + l'_w(w_{t-1}, x_t, y_t))$$

Thus, the stochastic gradient descent algorithm can be summarized in algorithm 3.1.

Algorithm 3.1

Initialize w_0

for t = 1, 2, ..., T

  Choose one sample (x_t, y_t) from A randomly

  Calculate w_t as:

  $$w_t = w_{t-1} - \eta_t S_t^{-1}(\lambda w_{t-1} + l'_w(w_{t-1}, x_t, y_t))$$

Output w_T

The number of iterations required to obtain a solution of accuracy ϵ is $O(1/\epsilon^2)$ [ZHA 04]. In 2007, Shalev-Shwartz *et al.* [SHA 07] modified the stochastic gradient descent algorithm, further improving the required number of iterations to reach the scale of $O(1/\epsilon)$. Moreover, the total run-time of the proposed method can be quantitatively recorded as $O(d/(\lambda\epsilon))$ where d is relevant to the number of non-zero features in each sample. Since this rate does not depend on the number of samples, this method is especially suitable for solving SVM on large-scale problems, even producing runtime decrease while the data size is increasing [SHA 08].

The new algorithm proposed by Shalev-Shwartz *et al.* is named Pegasos. It contains two main modifications on the previous stochastic gradient descent method. The first one is that, at each iteration, we choose k samples instead of only one sample for calculating subgradient. The other one is that, after updating w, we do one more step to project w on the L_2 ball of radius $1/\sqrt{\lambda}$.

At iteration t, after choosing a subset A_t which contains k samples from the training set A, the sublevel objective function can be written as:

$$f(w) = \frac{\lambda}{2}||w||^2 + \frac{1}{k} \sum_{(x,y) \in A_t} l(w, x, y)$$

Now, the variable updating rule includes two steps, one is normal gradient descent:

$$w_t = w_{t-1} - \eta_t f'_w(w_{t-1}) = (1 - \eta_t \lambda)w_{t-1} - \frac{\eta_t}{k} \sum_{(x,y) \in A_t} l'_w(w_{t-1}, x, y)$$

The other is scaling w_t by $\min\{1, \frac{1}{\sqrt{\lambda}||w_t||}\}$. The whole algorithm can be summarized in algorithm 3.2.

Algorithm 3.2

Input: A, λ, T, k

Initialize: Choose w_0 satisfies $||w_0|| \leq \frac{1}{\sqrt{\lambda}}$

for t = 1, 2, ..., T

Choose $A_t \subseteq A$, where $|A_t| = k$

Set learning rate $\eta_t = \frac{1}{\lambda t}$

Calculate $\hat{w}_t = (1 - \eta_t \lambda)w_{t-1} - \frac{\eta_t}{k} \sum_{(x,y) \in A_t} l'_w(w_{t-1}, x, y)$

Calculate $w_t = \min\{1, \frac{1}{\sqrt{\lambda}||\hat{w}_t||}\}\hat{w}_t$

Output w_T

In practice, if the loss function is defined as:

$$l(w, x, y) = \max\{0, 1 - y\langle w, x \rangle\},$$

then, it is only necessary to consider samples which have the attribute $y\langle w, x \rangle < 1$.

Each time, the k samples are chosen to be independent and identically distributed from the training set. Consider the extreme cases, if we choose $k = |A|$, then the algorithm becomes a subgradient projection method. In contrast, if we select $k = 1$, then we obtain a variant of the previous stochastic gradient descent method. Experimental results presented in [SHA 07] show that the projection operation can largely improve the convergence speed.

3.3.8. *Applications of support vector machines*

Since SVMs produce a strong generalization ability, they are becoming popular in a wide variety of application domains. This section briefly introduces some of them and shows how SVMs are applied to solve these problems.

One important task of the Internet application is automatic text categorization or what we call text classification. The aim is to automatically classify documents into predefined categories, such as classifying web pages into news, sports, science, health, technology, etc. Joachims first introduced SVMs in the application of text categorization [JOA 98]. In his work, each category, or we say each label, was treated as a binary classification problem. To collect the training data, each document was treated as a sample, and each distinct word was regarded as a feature. The value of the feature for each sample was the number of times the word occurs in this document. To reduce unnecessary features, the "stop words" such as "and", "or" and the words occurring fewer than three times were ignored. He also argued that SVMs were applicable in this application because they were essentially suitable to the properties of text which were high-dimensional feature spaces, few irrelevant features and sparse instance vectors. Experimental results showed that SVMs outperformed other learning algorithms, such as Bayes, Rocchio, C4.5 and k-NN, in both generalization ability and robustness. Since text can be classified automatically, we can use this technology in numerous applications. As concluded by Sebastiani and Ricerche [SEB 02], they could be automated indexing of scientific papers or patents, selective dissemination of information to customers, spam mail filtering, intrusion detection, authorship attribution, survey coding and even automated essay grading.

Another application field that broadly uses SVMs is computational biology [NOB 04, BEN 08], including remote protein homology detection, classification of genes, tissue, proteins and other microarray gene expression analysis, recognition of translation start sites, prediction of protein–protein interactions, functional classification of promoter regions and peptide identification from mass spectrometry data. Noble [NOB 04] explained why SVMs are successfully applied in these applications relevant to computational biology. First, these applications generally involve high-dimensional data with noises, for which SVMs perform well compared to other intelligent methods. Second, the kernel methods can easily handle different sorts of data, such as vectors, strings, trees, graphs, etc. These non-vector data types are common in biology applications, leading to the requirement of especially designed kernels, such as the Fisher kernel [JAA 99], composition-based kernel [DIN 01], Motif kernel [LOG 01], pairwise comparison kernel [LIA 03], etc.

SVMs have also been widely used in image processing. One of the important tasks is content-based image retrieval (CBIR). Much research has been carried out on using SVMs together with relevance feedback method in CBIR. The usual steps to achieve this purpose are as follows. First, we retrieve images through a traditional method, then user feeds back the top images in the retrieval result with relevance or irrelevance information to form the training data. Next, SVMs are trained and used to calculate scores for all of the images. Finally, the images are sorted according to their scores which reflect the relevance of the images to the user's requirements [ZHA 01]. Besides image retrieval, SVMs are also applied in image classification, segmentation, compression and other multimedia processing. These topics have attracted much more attention since multimedia content has been blooming on the Internet in recent years.

Other applications also benefit from the high-prediction performance of SVMs, such as E-learning, handwriting recognition, traffic prediction, two-dimensional (2-D) or three-dimensional (3-D) object detection, cancer diagnosis and prognosis, etc. A large amount of research is carried out on extensive SVMs in solving new problems – treating new applications, dealing with large-scale datasets and achieving active or online learning.

3.4. Concluding remarks

This chapter introduces two important AI models, artificial neural network and support vector machines, in detail. We investigated their principles and applications. Both of them have a number of variants, from simple models to complex high-level models, and show high ability to solve linear and nonlinear problems. There are many implementations of these models which are highly available in software depository nowadays. Some of them are commercial products and some are free tools or libraries. As we have discussed, when using these tools in training models, usually we need to design the architectures at first, such as choose how many layers and inner neurons for ANNs, evaluate and choose parameters for SVMs. This work is usually tedious. Fortunately, much research has been done on this topic and many effective methods have been proposed in last few decades.

Artificial Intelligence for Building Energy Analysis

4.1. Introduction

In this chapter, we apply artificial intelligence models in building energy analysis. There are two main applications, one is predicting energy consumption and the other is to perform faulty consumption detection and diagnosis. Both of them are crucial for energy conservation in building design, retrofit and operation as described in Chapter 1.

In the first application, we will investigate the performance of the SVR model in the prediction of energy consumption in the unknown future based on the historical behavior. Then, we try to extract models from multiple buildings' performance and carry out the prediction of the consumption for a new building. Two types of energy, electricity consumption and heating demand, will be used as the targets in the experiments. Furthermore, we will profoundly test the robustness of this model by considering various situations and try to find out in which circumstance the better performance is achieved. For this purpose, we design three sets of experiments that differ in the dataset selection, then analyze the trend of the model performance.

In the second application, we introduce an effective ANN model, RDP neural network, to implement fault detection and diagnosis (FDD) of building energy consumption. Based on the knowledge from previous faulty consumption, this model is able to report faults automatically and with a high accuracy. It also shows high performance in a newly designed fault diagnosis procedure.

Section 4.2.2 introduces some practical issues while applying SVM model. Sections 4.2.3 and 4.3 present the details of the two applications, prediction and fault detection, respectively. Finally, section 4.4 deals with conclusions and discussions.

4.2. Support vector machines for building energy prediction

4.2.1. *Energy prediction definition*

The function defined in equation [3.29] gives the model for predicting unknown targets with the new inputs x. Let us present what the prediction is on a real dataset. As shown in Table 4.1, the above is training data, which has full versions of features and targets, and is used to train the model. The data below indicates the new conditions in which targets are unknown and the prediction is to calculate the targets with the information composed of features. What we need is a high-performance model that can produce high prediction accuracy. To evaluate the model's performance, we use a test dataset where targets are already known. The model is run on the test dataset and produce predicted targets. By comparing the predicted targets and real targets through some statistical evaluation methods, we can report the model performance in terms of prediction accuracy.

Target	Temperature	Relative Humidity	Direct Solar	
721.71	13.3	80	27.2	...
738.11	13.9	78	37.1	...
762.93	14.7	74	57.2	...
792.23	15.6	70	77.5	...
818.36	16.9	76	82.9	...
851.80	18.8	79	83.2	...
...	...	...	...	...
?	12.5	85	37.2	...
?	13.1	76	22.3	...
?	14.2	71	69.2	...
?	17.7	72	58.6	...
?	...	...	...	...

Table 4.1. *Sample of dataset with the description of prediction*

Two methods are used to evaluate the model performance. One is the mean squared error (MSE), which gives the average deviation of the predicted values to the real values. The lower the MSE, the better the prediction performance. Suppose there are l testing samples, the decision function is $f(x)$ and the measured target is y, the MSE is defined as:

$$\text{MSE} = \frac{1}{l}\sum_{i=1}^{l}(f(x_i) - y_i)^2$$

The other method is the squared correlation coefficient (SCC), which lies in the range $[0, 1]$ and gives the ratio of successfully predicted number of target values on the total number of target values, i.e., how certain the predicted values are compared to the measured values. The higher the SCC, the stronger the prediction ability. Suppose there are l testing samples, the decision function is $f(x)$ and the measured target is y, the SCC is defined as:

$$\text{SCC} = \frac{(l\sum_{i=1}^{l} f(x_i)y_i - \sum_{i=1}^{l} f(x_i)\sum_{i=1}^{l} y_i)^2}{(l\sum_{i=1}^{l} f(x_i)^2 - (\sum_{i=1}^{l} f(x_i))^2)(l\sum_{i=1}^{l} y_i^2 - (\sum_{i=1}^{l} y_i)^2)}$$

4.2.2. *Practical issues*

This section discusses some important practical issues of applying SVR in building energy prediction. First, we introduce the steps of the operations, then we show how to preprocess the datasets and finally, we present the model selection.

4.2.2.1. *Operation flow*

In supervised learning theory, the experiments can be roughly divided into two steps, training and predicting. Accordingly, in order to evaluate the model, the dataset is divided into two sets, one is used for training, we call it a training set, and the other is used for predicting, called a testing set. A decision model is obtained in the training step based on the training set to indicate the dependence of the target on the features. In the predicting step, the derived model is applied on the testing set to predict the target values with regard to new features. By comparing the predicted target with the real one in the testing set through some statistical methods, it is possible to evaluate the prediction performance of the model.

The above steps that are necessary for our experiments are shown in Figure 4.1, where the historical consumption data are stored in the output file `output.txt`. It then becomes the input of this analyzing process. After dividing this dataset, we preprocess the two pieces of data (which will be introduced in section 4.2.2.3) and format them as training and testing sets. Before training the model, we have to select the right model components and set the parameters to appropriate values. How to do these things will be discussed in section 4.2.2.4.

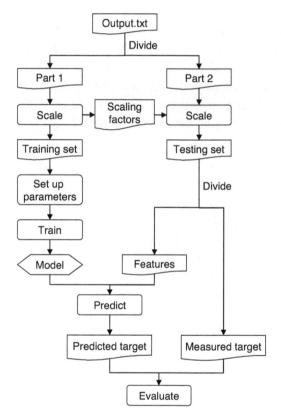

Figure 4.1. *Flow chart of a learning process*

4.2.2.2. *Experimental environment*

The hardware environment in the experiments is a workstation which has $8 * 2.5$ GHz CPU, 1,333 MHz FSB and 4G memory. The operating system is Linux with kernel version 2.6.

There are many SVM implementations both academically and commercially available to date. The Website [SVM 11] maintains a list of these pieces of software, including SVM-Light [JOA 99] and Libsvm [CHA 01], two widely used tools in the research community. They are well designed, efficient and have full implemented functions of SVM such as regression, classification and distribution estimation. They also provide elaborate description of the intrinsic mechanism and operating specifications. They are easy to learn and use. We choose Libsvm in our experiments since it was developed later than SVM-Light and it redesigned the superior features of this ancestor. It is intended to be a library and provides an interface to make it be easily integrated into other toolbox, such as Matlab, R and Weka. Its implementation is based on the sequential minimal optimization quadratic problem solver.

4.2.2.3. *Data preprocessing*

Before training SVR, we need to scale the values linearly into a small range in order to avoid numerical problems during the training procedure. Here, we chose the range $[0, 1]$. Suppose in the original training set, the value of jth dimension of sample i is v_{ij}, then the scaled value is given by the following simple formula:

$$\vec{v}_{ij} = \frac{v_{ij} - \min\{v_{kj}|k = 1, 2, ..., l\}}{\max\{v_{kj}|k = 1, 2, ..., l\} - \min\{v_{kj}|k = 1, 2, ..., l\}}$$

The target is also scaled into the same range. Moreover, the testing data should be scaled with the same scaling function as for the training set. Therefore, it is possible for the scaled testing values to be in a different range from that of the training values.

Since Libsvm is selected as the SVR implementation, the training data should be transformed into the format as required by this tool. Suppose there are 24 features, each sample should be in the following format:

$$T \quad 1 : v_1 \quad 2 : v_2 \quad 3 : v_3 \quad ... \quad 24 : v_{24}$$

4.2.2.4. *Model selection*

In our experiments, we select RBF as the kernel to train SVR models. Compared to other kernels, RBF is easier to use and very good in solving nonlinear problems. The parameters needed are C, ε and γ. The first two are for SVR and the last one is for RBF kernel. Choosing optimal values for these parameters is crucial in training a high-performance model. The best parameters should have the ability to well predict on unknown data without causing overfitting problem. In other words, the model should have high generalization ability as well as performing well on training set. For this purpose, the estimation of γ is obtained from

$$\gamma = \sum_{i,j=1}^{l} \left(\left\| x_i - x_j \right\|^2 \right)$$

as proposed in [TSA 05], where x_i and x_j are the feature values of ith and jth samples. The SVR parameters C and ε are solved by stepwise fivefold cross-validation on randomly selected subset of the training data. The initial searching spaces are $\{2^{-3}, 2^{-2}, ..., 2^8\}$ and $\{2^{-10}, 2^{-9}, ..., 2^{-5}\}$ for C and ε, respectively.

Let us show how the fivefold cross-validation works. First, we split the samples into five pieces uniformly as in Figure 4.2.

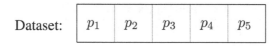

Dataset: | p_1 | p_2 | p_3 | p_4 | p_5 |

Figure 4.2. *Dataset*

Steps	Train on data	Test on data	Result
1	p_2, p_3, p_4, p_5	p_1	r_1
2	p_1, p_3, p_4, p_5	p_2	r_2
3	p_1, p_2, p_4, p_5	p_3	r_3
4	p_1, p_2, p_3, p_5	p_4	r_4
5	p_1, p_2, p_3, p_4	p_5	r_5

Table 4.2. *Training, testing and result*

Given a specific (C, ε) pair, we train and test the model five times on the pieces as Table 4.2 shows, and choose the best performance from $\{r_1, r_2, r_3, r_4, r_5\}$ as the final result for this pair. Then, we go to the next pair of (C, ε) and run the same process. We repeat this procedure until all of the possible pairs are evaluated. Finally, we are able to pick up the optimal pair that produces the best accuracy. This is exactly what we need in the later model training.

4.2.3. *Support vector machines for prediction*

In this section, three sets of experiments are going to be performed. The first one aims to test how the performance of SVR is in the prediction of a single building's energy consumption, including two main types of energy: heating demand and electricity. In order to investigate the model's robustness, we design the second set of experiments where the models are trained on a different period of historical consumption, and the influence of the training data size is fully studied. This set of experiments is still based on a single office building. Later, in the third experiment, we train the SVR model in multiple buildings and test the performance of this model in the prediction of a completely new building. The data used for model training and testing is simulated in EnergyPlus as described in Chapter 2. The models in the three sets of experiments are trained on different types of datasets.

4.2.3.1. *Prediction of single building energy*

In winter, the buildings in France consume large amounts of district heating. In the first model development, the district heating consumption data are gathered hourly from a single building in the heating season, i.e. from November 1 to March 31. There are 3,624 samples with 24 features in the final dataset. We take the samples of the last 2 days as testing set, and the rest of them for training use. Therefore, the number of training samples is 3,576 and that of testing samples is 48. The parameters of the SVR model are set as $C = 16$, $\gamma = 0.7533$ and $\varepsilon = 0.01$ by the method described in section 4.2.2.4. The final result of the prediction is plotted in Figure 4.3 where the predicted and actual targets are shown together. We can see that the two curves fit very well, which means that the model has a very good generalization performance. Actually, the number of SVs is 2,229 and MSE and SCC are 2.3×10^{-3} and 0.927918, respectively. We also can see the good performance from these evaluation methods.

Another important type of energy consumed by buildings is electricity. We also train the SVR model to predict this type of energy. To be different from the previous experiment, this time we choose the consumption data through 1 whole year, and the testing dataset, which contains 48 samples, is randomly selected from the global dataset. The features are the same as in the first experiment. The number of training samples is 8,712. The parameters are set as $C = 16$, $\gamma = 0.3043$ and $\varepsilon = 0.01$. The results show that there are 2,126 support vectors, MSE is equal to 5.27×10^{-4}, and SCC is equal to 0.959905. The model performs even better in this case. The measured and predicted values are plotted in Figure 4.4. In most cases, the two curves fit well except at 18 and 27 hr.

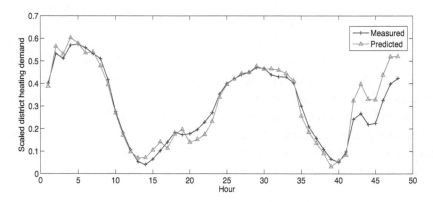

Figure 4.3. *Measured and predicted district heating demand in heating season. For a color version of this figure, see www.iste.co.uk/magoules/mining.zip*

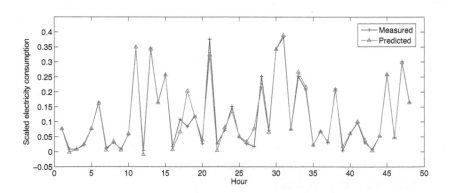

Figure 4.4. *Measured and predicted electricity consumption in randomly selected 48 hr. For a color version of this figure, see www.iste.co.uk/magoules/mining.zip*

4.2.3.2. *Extensive model evaluation*

The size of training dataset has a certain influence on the model's performance. In the previous section, the first model is trained on 5 months' data, whereas the second model is trained on 1 year's data, and we see that the second prediction fits better than the first prediction. However, in the second training process, the testing data are drawn randomly from the whole dataset, this indicates that the characteristic of the testing samples is quite close to that of the training samples. In contrast, in the first training process, since the testing and the training datasets are for different days, they are more different in characteristics. In order to sufficiently study the model's performance in this application, we design the following experiments that vary in training and testing datasets.

Three models are trained. Training the testing datasets are described in Table 4.3. We choose electricity as the target since we have these data for a whole year.

Train on data	Test on data
January	March, April, ..., December
January - April	June, July, ..., December
January - August	September, October, November, December

Table 4.3. *Consumption period for the training and testing datasets*

The first model is trained on the consumption of only 1 month (January), then we use the derived model to predict the consumptions in other months (from February to December). To see the performance of the prediction on these months that are totally different from the training month, we selected 4 months to draw the predicted errors, which is defined as measured values minus predicted values. They are March, May, July and September, as shown in Figure 4.5. The MSE and SCC of all of the months (from March to December) are shown in Figures 4.8 and 4.9, respectively. We can see an obvious convex trend of the prediction accuracy, i.e. March, November and December hold the best performance while July is the worst. This is due to the reason that the previous 3 months are in winter is the same as January: In other words, the characteristics of the first 3 months, such as weather conditions and HVAC service, are similar as that in January. In contrast, July is in summer, it is the most different month from January.

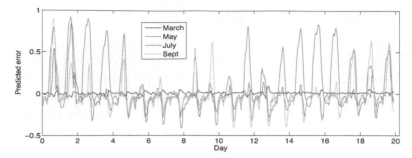

Figure 4.5. *Prediction error of the model on the consumption of March, May, July and September. The model is trained on the data of January. For a color version of this figure, see www.iste.co.uk/ magoules/mining.zip*

The second model is trained on the consumption from January to April, which is 3 months more than the first training set. The prediction is tested on each month from May to December. We also draw 4 months' prediction errors in order for the readers to have a global view of the model's performance, as shown in Figure 4.6. The MSE and SCC are also shown in Figures 4.8 and 4.9. We still can see that in July the model has the worst performance, whereas in December it has the best performance. Another important thing is that from June to October, the present model performance is better than the previous performance whose training data contain only January. This case indicates that sufficient data are important for training a good model.

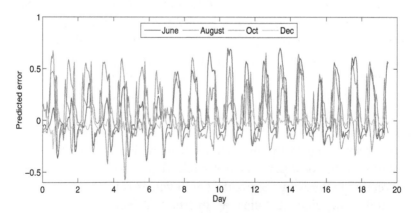

Figure 4.6. *Prediction error of the model on the consumption of June, August, October and December. The model is trained on the data from January to April. For a color version of this figure, see www.iste.co.uk/magoules/mining.zip*

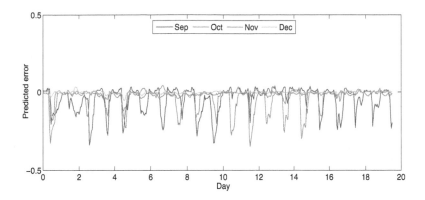

Figure 4.7. *Prediction error of the model on the consumption of September, October, November and December. The model is trained on the data from January to August. For a color version of this figure, see www.iste.co.uk/magoules/mining.zip*

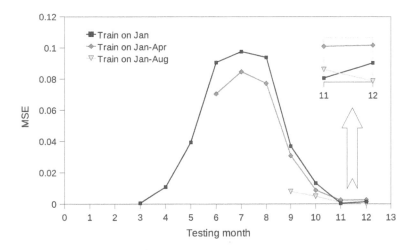

Figure 4.8. *Mean squared error of the three models on the designed testing months. For a color version of this figure, see www.iste.co.uk/magoules/mining.zip*

In the third model training, we enlarge the training data period by using the consumption from January to August, 4 more months than the previous months. Then, the model is applied on each month between September and December. Again, we draw 4 months' results in Figure 4.7, and show MSE and SCC in Figures 4.8 and 4.9, respectively. We can see that, in September and

December, the present prediction accuracy is better than that of the previous two models. This indicates that the greater the training data, the better the model's performance. However, this is not always true. At least in November, the model is not as good as the first one. Note that the first model only has 1-month of data for training, which is far less than the present model.

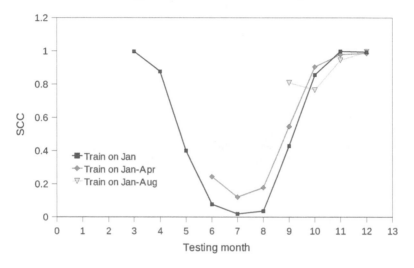

Figure 4.9. *Squared correlation coefficient of the three models on the designed testing months. For a color version of this figure, see www.iste.co.uk/magoules/mining.zip*

4.2.3.3. *Prediction of multiple buildings energy*

The above learning processes are based on the energy consumption of a single building and the evaluation of the model is to predict the unknown future in the same building. In practice, it is quite useful to predict how much energy is required in a completely new building. Therefore, in the second experiment, we tried to learn a model based on the energy data where the building structures are involved. That is to say, we trained a model from the consumption behaviors of several buildings, then applied the model to predict the behavior of a totally different building. In this experiment, 100 buildings are simulated in the heating season. They are under the same weather conditions but have different properties, such as different orientations, volumes, people densities and fenestration. We chose the data of the first 99 buildings as the training set and data of the last building as the testing set. The number of features is 28. The number of training samples is 358,776, and the number of testing samples is 3,624. The model parameters are set as $C = 4$, $\gamma = 0.3179$ and $\varepsilon = 0.01$. In the training step, the number of SVs is 27,501, while in the predicting step, MSE is 5.01×10^{-5} and SCC is 0.997639. The predicted and measured values on the first 100 samples in test dataset are plotted in Figure 4.10. The results show us that SVR has a very good prediction performance in building energy consumption when building diversity is taken into account. It provides us the possibility to predict the energy performance of a building for designing as well as for retrofitting.

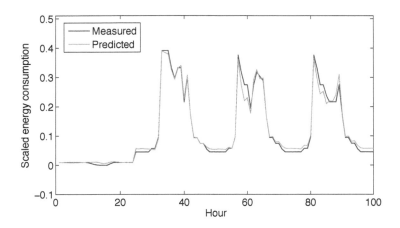

Figure 4.10. *Measured and predicted electricity consumption for a totally new building. The model is trained on 99 buildings. For a color version of this figure, see www.iste.co.uk/magoules/mining.zip*

4.3. Neural networks for fault detection and diagnosis

In recent decades, FDD for building energy consumption has been widely and thoroughly investigated. In the previous work, various system levels have been considered: from subsystem equipment to whole building levels, mainly including air-handling units (AHUs), air-conditioning systems, vapor compression systems and higher level systems such as the HVAC system. A large number of advanced methods or techniques were proposed and utilized, such as simulation, ANNs PCA, residual analysis, fuzzy model, transient pattern analysis, SVMs, expert rule-based method and hybrid method.

The most direct approach for fault detection is to calculate normal consumption and then compare it with the measured real one. A fault can be reported whenever they are not consistent and exceed a certain threshold. The calculation for this purpose can be accomplished by the engineering method or simulation, such as in [LIU 02, SON 03, NOR 02].

ANNs are well applicable to distinguish normal and abnormal energy consumptions due to their classification ability. Lee *et al.* [LEE 97] have introduced an ANN for FDD of an AHU. This method has been used to treat eleven faults including fan failure and sensor failure. Bailey and Kreider [BAI 03] have used ANN to FDD of chillers. Tassou and Grace [TAS 05] have applied ANNs for the FDD purpose in vapor compression refrigeration systems. Du *et al.* [DU 10] have used a dynamic fuzzy neural approach to perform fault diagnosis for an AHU. Lee *et al.* [LEE 04] have proposed the general regression neural networks to detect faults in sensor values and control signals for AHUs. These faults were determined when residuals exceeded predefined thresholds. In the case where residuals are small, detection might be inaccurate. To solve this problem, Yang *et al.* [YAN 11] have suggested to adopt fractal correlation dimension deviation instead of the direct residual. They showed that this novel method was able to detect relatively small bias fault under noise conditions.

PCA was adopted by Du *et al.* [DU 10] and Wang *et al.* [WAN 04] in fault diagnosis for air dampers, variable air volume (VAV) terminals and AHUs. An expert-based multivariate decoupling method has been proposed in [XIA 06, XIA 09] for the purpose to enhance the capability of the PCA-based method in fault diagnosis of AHUs.

Liang and Du [LIA 07] have used the residual analysis method to detect three faults in a HVAC system, i.e. recirculation damper stuck, cooling coil fouling/block and supply fan speed decreasing. A multilayer SVM classifier has therefore been developed to diagnose these three kinds of faults. For improving performance, Han *et al.* [HAN 11] have adopted a feature selection technique using multiclass SVM as a FDD tool for chillers.

Schein *et al.* [SCH 06] have used 28 expert rules, which were derived from mass and energy balances, to serve the purpose of fault detection in AHUs. Kim and Kim [KIM 05] have used two different rule-based modules for an easy diagnosis of faults in the vapor compression system.

Several hybrid approaches took advantage of two or more effective models, achieving both higher flexibility and suitability. Qin and

Wang [QIN 05] have proposed a hybrid method that combines expert rules, performance indexes and statistical process control models, in the implementation of FDD for 10 faults in air-conditioning systems. Also for air-conditioning systems, Hou *et al.* [HOU 06b] have combined data mining, a rough set approach and an ANN model for sensor fault detection and diagnosis. Norford *et al.* [NOR 02] have applied two methods for FDD in HVAC equipment. One was based on first principles models of system components, the other was based on semi-empirical correlations of submetered electrical power with flow rates or process control signals. Namburu *et al.* [NAM 07] developed a generic FDD scheme for centrifugal chillers, in which fault classification techniques were chosen from support vector machines, principal component analysis and partial least squares. House *et al.* [HOU 99] have compared five models in detecting and diagnosing seven faults of an AHU system, i.e. ANN, nearest neighbor, nearest prototype classifier, rule-based classifier and Bayes classifier.

Certain approaches are less used compared with the approaches mentioned earlier. A fuzzy model has been used by Dexter and Ngo [DEX 01] in fault diagnosis of air-conditioning systems. A transient pattern analysis approach has been proposed by Cho *et al.* [CHO 05] for FDD of fan, sensor and damper. An easy-to-use FDD method has been developed by Song *et al.* [SON 08] for the whole building air-conditioning system based on indoor air temperature changes. A spatial-temporal partition strategy has been proposed by Wu and Sun [WU 11] to allow cross-level FDD for HVAC systems, such as detecting faults on the AHU level and VAV level. A bond graph model has been proposed by Ghiaus [GHI 99] for FDD in the air-conditioning system. A dynamic adaptive model and operating variable dynamic thresholds have been adopted by Navarro [NAV 06a] to detect real-time faults in chillers.

However, system level FDD still needs further improvement. Although several techniques have already been adopted, a more reliable and accurate model is always required. This section proposes an alternative and highly effective approach [MAG 13], which is based on RDP neural network for solving FDD in the system level. RDP is effective since it is designed to be able to report 100% correct classification on a testing dataset. The chosen data include certain real-time physical variables that are measured by sensors and meters installed throughout the building. In addition, a new architecture of diagnosing the detected faults is proposed. Given a sample of faulty consumption, it is able to point out which piece of electric equipment causes this fault. Furthermore, it can list all of the possible causes in the descending probability order, making it easy to deal with broader problems. This method is based on the evaluation of several RDP models, each of which is designed to be able to detect unique device fault. Fortunately, experimental results show that this method can diagnose faults correctly.

4.3.1. *Description of faults*

Faults are caused by the use of inefficient control and operational sequences, and the existence of system faults. The following are some typical HVAC system faults and their identification procedures. Two of the seven faults are related to terminal box reheat valves and minimum box airflow. The other five faults considered involve AHU minimum outside airflow, outside air damper quality, maximum supply airflow, static pressure control and building positive pressure control.

– *Terminal box reheat valve leakage*: many of the terminal boxes in buildings are located with difficulty in accessing and maintaining. Reheat coil control valve leakage often causes unnecessary simultaneous heating and cooling energy consumption. For example, 10% water leakage in a reheat coil may increase heating and cooling cost in that zone by 50%. This unwanted heat supplied to the air stream can also cause comfort problems during summer.

– *Improper minimum terminal box airflow*: the minimum airflow through terminal boxes is a critical parameter affecting indoor air quality (IAQ), air circulation and energy consumption. If the minimum airflow is higher than required, it often leads to significant simultaneous heating and cooling, in addition to excessive fan power. If minimum flow is less than required, it may cause IAQ problems and lack of air circulation.

– *Improper minimum outside airflow*: this is critical to controlling the minimum outside air intake. If it is higher than required, excess energy is used to condition the outside air. If it is too low, IAQ problems will appear. When the outside airflow is not monitored and modulated, the outside air intake is dependent on the total airflow.

– *Poor outside air damper quality*: when an economizer is designed and installed, the outside air dampers often have a significant cross-sectional area. The air leakage with the damper closed may be higher than the required minimum outside air if poor dampers are used or the mixing chamber has excessive negative pressure.

– *Excessive maximum supply airflow*: for a constant air volume system, excessive maximum airflow often causes the following problems: (1) excessive fan power, (2) excessive cooling and heating, (3) high humidity and (4) excessive noise.

– *Improper supply air static pressure*: for VAV systems, the fan speed is often controlled for the purpose to maintain the static pressure at the position 2/3 downstream in the main duct at a preselected value. This value is often specified by design engineers during the design phase. If this value is too low, some of the terminal boxes may not be able to provide adequate airflow to the spaces. Therefore, an excessive value is often specified. When excessively high static pressure is used, it creates noise in the terminal boxes, consumes more fan power than necessary and causes excessive thermal energy use as well.

– *Improper building positive pressure*: building positive pressure control is critical for IAQ control, moisture damage prevention in humid climates and building thermal comfort.

4.3.2. *RDP in fault detection*

This section deals with detection of building energy consumption faults using selected variables. RDP classification models have been developed and tested for buildings with various electric systems and distinct fault regimes. This has been done to analyze the applicability and robustness of the RDP models to detect faults in diverse system domains.

4.3.2.1. *Introduce faults to the simulated building*

In our experiments, the daily electricity consumption is considered as the energy form. An office building in France is simulated with EnergyPlus.

The consumption is recorded over a year, i.e. from November 1 to March 31. The description of this building is shown in Table 4.4. More details, such as three layers of materials of surfaces, are ignored for simplicity reason. Note that these materials that determine the thermal behavior of the building envelope have significant influence on the total energy consumption. Descriptions of these materials can be found in the documents of EnergyPlus [ENE 11].

Parameters	Values
Location	Paris-orly, urban area
Duration	From Jan 1 to Dec 31
Time Step	15 min
Building Shape	Rectangle
Structure	Length: 11
	Width: 10
	Ceiling Height: 4
	North axis: 10°
Fenestration Surface	14 m^2 for each wall
Thermal Zones	5
People	14
Air Infiltration	0.0348 m^3/s
Heating Type	Heat pump
Cooling Type	Centrale Chiller

Table 4.4. *Description of a single building (in metric units)*

For the sake of simplicity, we suppose there is only one floor and one room in this building. In heating season, the energy consumed in this building mainly comes from three sources: the district heating that is used to keep the inside temperature at a constant level, electricity plants that are used mostly on working days and hot water for office use. For the walls in each orientation, there are several construction layers due to thermal considerations. This requires three layers of materials in the walls. The roof is in the same condition. The open/close time of the building and schedules of the inner equipment are carefully set as for normal office purposes in France.

The building is equipped with a HVAC system. The designed heating type is heat pump and cooling type is central chiller. We introduce these electric devices into the building in order to verify whether or not the faults caused by them can be detected. The inner electrical plants that might cause consumption errors are lights, fan, coil, pump and chiller.

The run period for the simulation is 1 year. The recording is dumped daily. The output variables that are selected for detection of abnormality in the building energy consumption are listed in the following; their units are Joules:

– *Facility electric consumption (FEC)*: this is the accumulated electric consumption of the building zones, the plant loops, the air loops, the interior as well as exterior electric equipment.

– *Interior equipment electric consumption*: this includes all of the interior equipment in all zones.

– *Cooling electric consumption*: this stands for the electric consumption for cooling purpose.

– *Fans electricity consumption*: this is the electric power input to the fans.

– *Pumps electricity consumption*: this is the electric power input to the heat pumps.

– *Chiller electric consumption*: this is the electric power input to the chiller.

The parameters of these electric equipment are set to default values in EnergyPlus, indicating normal usage, and 1-year long simulation is performed to generate normal conditions. After that, faults are introduced to this building, and once again, 1-year long faulty consumption is simulated. The faults are introduced by changing performance parameters of equipment in order to reflect their performance degradation. We select six parameters of four equipment and decrease 35% of their performance. They are listed in Table 4.5. The first column lists equipment that might cause detectable consumption errors. The second column gives the performance parameters of the corresponding equipment. The third column is the performance degradation from normal usage to faulty condition.

Equipment	Parameter	Change
Fan	Fan efficiency	$0.6 \rightarrow 0.39$
	Motor efficiency	$0.9 \rightarrow 0.59$
Coil	Design water flow rate	$0.0022 \rightarrow 0.003 \ m^3/s$
Pump	Motor efficiency	$0.9 \rightarrow 0.59$
Chiller	Reference COP	$3 \rightarrow 1.95$

Table 4.5. *Faults introduced to the building*

Although performance degradation is set to equipment, the building is not always in faulty usage. In reality, there are quite number of days that the equipment are not used frequently. In these cases, the consumption changes are not obvious and undetectable. Therefore, the whole year profiles with faults introduced cannot be simply considered as faulty usage (or we say errors). Based on the generated normal and faulty datasets, we set a threshold to determine whether or not a sample is a real error. The threshold will determine the number of errors in the final datasets. Here, we simply choose 1,000 J. If the consumption change in current day is less than 1,000 J, then this day is still considered as a normal condition. Otherwise, it is considered as a fault. In the final datasets, each normal sample is assigned with a label "1" while faulty samples are labeled "0".

To have an overview of consumption changes after introducing faults, we depict FEC in 1 year, as shown in Figure 4.11. We can see an obvious consumption increase in most of the days when faults are introduced.

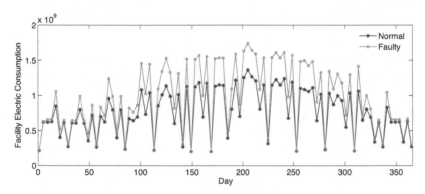

Figure 4.11. *Normal and faulty facility electric consumption in 1 year (the unit is Joules (J)). For a color version of this figure, see www.iste.co.uk/magoules/mining.zip*

4.3.2.2. *Experiments and results*

Based on above datasets, two experiments are designed to test the ability of RDP model in fault detection. In the first, 10 months normal and 10 months faulty data are combined to train the model and the combination of remaining 2 months data is used for testing. In the second, only 6 months' data are used for training and the remaining 6 months data are used for testing. The number of samples of these datasets are shown in Table 4.6. The number of features is six for all of the datasets.

Experiment I		Experiment II	
Training set	Testing set	Training set	Testing set
610	120	365	365

Table 4.6. *Number of samples in the datasets*

The experiments are performed on a dual-core computer with 2.4G*2 CPU, 2G memory and windows XP installed. The testing results are shown in Table 4.7. We can see that the prediction accuracy is very high. On the first testing set, which contains 2 months' consumption, it achieves 100%. On 6 months set, it reaches as high as 97.81%. On both training sets, the accuracy remains 100% as the model is designed to achieve.

	Experiment I	Experiment II
Time (s)	13.78	8
Model size	9	9
Accuracy on training set (%)	100	100
Accuracy on testing set (%)	100	97.81

Table 4.7. *Results of recursive deterministic perceptron model in two experiments*

In the above faulty consumption dataset, performance of four equipment degraded at the same time as described in Table 4.5. We see the model is very effective in this extreme case. However, how the model performance would be if there is only one degraded equipment? Intuitively, a unique decrease in the performance of equipment would cause the deviation of normal and abnormal consumption less obvious. We simulate four datasets, each of them contains faulty consumption caused by only one equipment. Then, we train and test RDP models on these four sets combined with normal consumption dataset. Like the previous experiment I, we train on 10 months and test on 2 months. Table 4.8 presents the results. We can see the accuracy is still very high, indicating that RDP is effective in detecting faults of one equipment.

	On training set	On testing set
Fan	100	99.22
Coil	100	97.29
Pump	100	97.32
Chiller	100	97.30

Table 4.8. *Recursive deterministic perceptron model accuracy (%) on datasets in four cases. Ten months for training and two months for testing. Each dataset contains normal consumption with faults caused by one equipment, indicated in the first column*

4.3.3. *RDP in fault diagnosis*

Here, we propose a new method to identify the faulty equipment that causes the detected abnormal consumption. Considering the above building, suppose the possible sources of faults are the chiller, coil, fan or pump, we denote them as E_1, E_2, E_3 and E_4, respectively. What we want is a procedure that can tell us which equipment works abnormally when given faulty consumption. An even better result is a list of equipment in the order of fault risk, since more than one equipment might be wrong simultaneously. If such kind of list is provided, then we can easily know that which one is the most possible source of the fault and which one is the second, third and so on.

Let us solve this problem. Four models are trained in order to predict errors caused by each single source, denoted by M_1, M_2, M_3 and M_4. One requirement is that each model can predict errors only caused by the corresponding source and it reports errors caused by other sources as normal situations. For instance, M_3 can only detect fan (E_3) errors and would report errors caused by the chiller, coil or pump as normal consumption. If this requirement is satisfied, then we can use the procedure depicted in Figure 4.12 to isolate the faulty equipment. It works as follows. Given some faulty samples, which can be detected by RDP models as discussed in the previous section, we input them to the four models and record their prediction accuracy, then the order of possible faulty equipment is exactly the descending order of these four accuracies. The reason is that, when the prediction accuracy of M_i is high, the input faulty samples are more like the training profiles of M_i, thus these faulty samples are more likely to be caused by the corresponding equipment E_i, rather than other equipment.

Now the problem is how to train these models to make them only sensitive to their corresponding degradation of equipment. The solution is simple. The only thing we need to do is to make it so that the models predicting errors caused by other sources appear as normal situations. To implement this idea, suppose we have four faulty datasets, each of which contains one faulty equipment, then we create training dataset for each model as follows. We use an example to explain this procedure. Suppose we want to create training data for model M_1, we pick up the faulty samples from the faulty dataset that contains E_1 degradation, associate them with label "0" and put in the training dataset. Then, we extract faulty samples from other three datasets, associate them with label "1" and put them together into the training set. This means in generating model M_1, and we consider faults caused by E_2, E_3 and E_4 as normal samples. Finally, the model is trained on this dataset and is expected to be only sensitive to E_1 degradation.

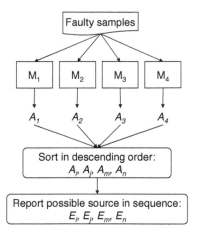

Figure 4.12. *Flow chart of fault diagnosis. M_i is the ith model, A_i is the prediction accuracy through the ith model and E_i stands for the ith equipment*

One experiment is designed to test the proposed method. First, we generate four faulty datasets under EnergyPlus to indicate degradation of four equipment, with the parameters setting as described in Table 4.5. Then, we use the above method to prepare four RDP models. The data for model training are the first 10 months' profiles. Then, we implement the procedure as described in Figure 4.12 and verify that whether or not this method can report the right faulty equipment. The chiller is chosen as the example. The input faulty samples are the remaining two months faulty consumption data when the chiller fault is introduced. The accuracy of the four models on this testing dataset is shown in Table 4.9. It is easy to know the sequence of the possible faulty equipment, i.e. $E_1 > E_3 > E_4 > E_2$, and the accuracy of E_1 is obviously higher than that of others. Therefore, we can easily judge that the chiller is the most likely source of the fault. This method reports exactly the right answer.

A_1	A_2	A_3	A_4
94.12	1.96	11.76	5.88

Table 4.9. *Recursive deterministic perceptron model accuracy in the diagnostic procedure with the example inputs*

4.4. Concluding remarks

This chapter applies SVR in the prediction of building energy consumption. We demonstrate the performance of this model in extensive experiments, representing various situations, such as single/multiple buildings, electricity/district heating consumptions, small/large training sets and close/far away of the training and testing profiles. SVR shows very high generalization ability and robustness in these tests.

Then, the RDP neural network model is used to detect and diagnose faults in the whole building level systems. Four pieces of equipment in normal and abnormal conditions are simulated to evaluate this model. Experiments demonstrate that this model show high accuracy in detecting all possible faults, including one equipment degradation and all four equipment degradation. More specifically, on training set, the accuracy is 100% and on testing set it reaches higher than 97%.

Based on the high detection ability of RDP, we proposed a new fault diagnostic architecture. Other than correctly report source of faults, it can list the equipment in order, according to their possibilities of occurring malfunction. This attribute allows us to diagnose faults caused by more than one source. Even, we are able to deal with the problem in which several equipment cause similar faults.

In the following chapters, we will evaluate this model on real consumption data, test other classification models and compare their performance. In addition, we will investigate how to parallelize this model to achieve higher performance.

5

Model Reduction for Support Vector Machines

5.1. Introduction

In Chapter 1, we stated that there are a great number of factors which probably impact energy dynamics of a building. In Chapter 4, when predicting one single building's energy profiles, we selected 24 features to train the model, including variables from weather conditions, energy profiles of each sublevel component, ventilation, water temperature, etc. While predicting multiple buildings' consumption, four more features which represent building structure characteristics were used. However, we do not guarantee that these features are the right choices, nor can we even say they are all useful. How to reasonably choose a subset of appropriate features to be used in model learning is one of the key issues in machine learning. On the one hand, using different sets of features would probably change the performance of the models in accuracy and learning speed. On the other hand, the optimal set of features would make the predictive models more practical.

In this chapter, we discuss how to select subsets of features for SVR applied to the prediction of building energy consumption [ZHA 12a]. We present a heuristic approach for selecting subsets of features in this chapter, and systematically analyze how it will influence the model performance. The motivation is to develop a feature set that is simple enough and can be recorded easily in practice. The models are trained by SVR with different kernel methods based on three datasets. The model reduction or the feature selection (FS) method is evaluated by comparing the models' performances before and after FS is performed.

This chapter is organized as follows. Section 5.2 gives an overview of model reduction, and introduces three directions of feature selection. Section 5.3 discusses general FS methods and in particular the ones introduced in this work. Sections 5.4 and 5.5 illustrate, with several numerical experiments, the robustness and efficiency of the proposed method. Finally, section 5.6 gives the conclusion and discussion.

5.2. Overview of model reduction

The past few years have witnessed the significant change in data sciences, where domains with hundreds to tens of thousands of variables or features are being thoroughly explored. Two typical examples of these new application domains are shown here, which serve us as an illustration of this introduction. One is gene selection from microarray data and the other is text categorization. For the former, the variables are gene expression coefficients corresponding to the abundance of mRNA in a sample, e.g. tissue biopsy, for a certain number of patients. A typical classification task is to separate healthy patients from those with cancer, based on their gene expression profiles. Under normal circumstances, fewer than 100 examples (patients) are available altogether for training and testing. However, in reality, the number of variables in the raw data ranges from 6,000 to 60,000. Certain initial filtering usually renders this number to a few thousand. For the reason that the abundance of mRNA varies by several orders of magnitude depending on the gene, the variables are usually standardized. In the text classification problem, documents are represented by a bag-of-words, which is a vector of dimension with a size of the vocabulary containing word frequency counts (proper normalization of the variables also applies). Common vocabularies usually carry hundreds of thousands of words, so that an initial pruning of the most and least frequent words may significantly reduce the effective number of words to 15,000. Furthermore, large document collections of 5,000 to 800,000 documents are also available for research. Typical tasks include the automatic sorting of URLs into a web directory and the detection of unsolicited emails (spam).

New techniques are being developed to address these challenging tasks, where many irrelevant and redundant variables are involved often with comparatively fewer training examples. Obvious potential benefits of variable and feature selection are facilitating data visualization and data understanding, reducing the measurement and storage requirements, reducing training and utilization time, and defying the curse of dimensionality for improving prediction performance. Generally, they are divided into wrappers, filters and embedded methods. Wrappers use the learning machine of interest as a black box to score subsets of variables according to their predictive power. Filters select subsets of variables as a preprocessing step, independently of the chosen predictor. Embedded methods perform variable selection in the training process and are usually specific to the given learning machines.

5.2.1. *Wrapper methods*

This method offers a simple and powerful way to address the problem of variable selection, regardless of the chosen learning machine. In fact, the learning machine is considered as a perfect black box and the method lends itself to the use of off-the-shelf machine-learning software packages. In its most general formulation, the wrapper methodology consists of using the prediction performance of a given learning machine to assess the relative usefulness of subsets of variables. In practice, we need to define: (1) how to search the space of all possible variable subsets; (2) how to assess the prediction performance of a learning machine for the purpose of guiding the search or halting it; and (3) which predictor to choose. Generally, an exhaustive search can conceivably be performed, provided that the number of variables is not too large. However, this problem is known to be NP-hard [AMA 98] and the search correspondingly becomes quickly computationally intractable. Therefore, in tackling this problem, a wide range of search strategies is proposed, which includes best-first, branch-and-bound, simulated annealing and genetic algorithms. Their performance assessments are usually implemented by using a validation set or by cross-validation. As illustrated here, popular predictors include decision trees, naive bayes, least-square linear predictors and support vector machines.

Wrappers are often criticized as being a brute force method requiring massive amounts of computation, which is not always the case. More efficient search strategies are, therefore, devised. The use of such strategies is not necessarily at the expense of prediction performance. In fact, it appears to be the inverse in some cases: coarse search strategies may alleviate the problem of overfitting. Greedy search strategies seem to be particularly computationally advantageous and robust against overfitting. They run well in both forward selection and backward elimination. For the former one, variables are progressively incorporated into larger and larger subsets, whereas for the latter one, it starts with the set of all variables and progressively eliminates the least promising ones. Both methods yield nested subsets of variables. On the one hand, by using the learning machine as a black box, wrappers are remarkably universal and simple. On the other hand, embedded methods that incorporate variable selection as a part of the training process may be more efficient in the following several respects: they make better use of the available data in the sense that they do not need to split the training data into a training and validation set; they reach a solution faster by avoiding retraining a predictor from scratch for every variable subset investigated. Embedded methods are not new, decision trees such as classification and regression trees (CARTs), for instance, have a built-in mechanism to perform variable selection. The next two sections are devoted to two families of embedded methods illustrated by algorithms.

5.2.2. *Filter methods*

Certain justifications for using filters in subset selection have been put forward. It is argued that filters are faster compared to wrappers. Moreover, recently proposed efficient embedded methods are competitive in this respect. Another argument is that some filters, e.g. those based on mutual information criteria, provide a generic selection of variables, not tuned for/by a given learning machine. A third compelling justification suggested that filtering can be used as a preprocessing step to reduce space dimensionality and overcome overfitting. In this respect, it seems reasonable to use a wrapper (or embedded method) with a linear predictor as the filter and then train a more complex nonlinear predictor on the resulting variables. A classic example of this approach is found in the paper of Bi *et al.* [BI 03]: a linear 1-norm SVM is used for variable selection, while a nonlinear 1-norm SVM is used for prediction. The complexity of linear filters can be ramped up by adding to the selection process products of input variables (monomials of a polynomial) and retaining the variables that are part of any selected monomial. Another predictor, e.g. a neural network, is eventually substituted to the polynomial to perform predictions using the selected variables. In some cases, however, we may want to reduce the complexity of linear filters to overcome overfitting problems. When the number of examples is small compared to the number of variables (for instance, in the case of microarray data), we may need to resort to selecting variables with correlation coefficients. Information theoretic filtering methods such as Markov blanket algorithms contribute to another broad family. The justification for classification problems is that the measure of mutual information does not rely on any prediction process, but provides a bound on the error rate with any prediction scheme for the given distribution. No illustration of such methods is provided for the problem of variable subset selection.

5.2.3. *Embedded methods*

Embedded methods are very different from other feature selection methods in how feature selection and learning interact. Unlike the wrapper methods, filter methods do not incorporate learning. Wrapper methods use a learning machine to measure the quality of subsets of features without incorporating knowledge about the specific structure of the classification or regression function, and can therefore be combined with any learning machine. In contrast to filter or wrapper approaches, in embedded methods the learning part and the feature selection part cannot be separated – the structure of the class of functions under consideration plays a crucial role. There are three embedded methods:

– *Explicit removal or addition of features*: the scaling factors are optimized over the discrete set $\{0, 1\}^n$ in a greedy iteration;

– *Optimization of scaling factors*: the optimization is performed over the compact interval $[0, 1]^n$;

– *Linear approaches*: these approaches directly enforce sparsity of the model parameters.

Each family of feature selection methods, i.e. filter, wrapper and embedded, has its own advantages and drawbacks. In general, filter methods are fast, since they do not incorporate learning. Most wrapper methods are slower compared to filter methods, since they typically need to evaluate a cross-validation scheme at every iteration. Whenever the function that measures the quality of a scaling factor can be evaluated faster than a cross-validation error estimation procedure, embedded methods are, therefore, expected to be faster than wrapper approaches. Embedded methods tend to have higher capacity than filter methods and are therefore more likely to overfit. We thus expect filter methods to perform better if only small amounts of training data are available. While as the number of training points increases, embedded methods will eventually outperform filter methods.

5.3. Model reduction for energy consumption

5.3.1. *Introduction*

FS is a challenging subject and is widely studied in the machine-learning community. PCA and KPCA are two broadly used methods in exploratory data analysis and training predictive models [ROS 01]. In a raw dataset, there would be correlations between variables. PCA aims at reducing these correlations and making variance of data as high as possible. It converts a set of possibly correlated features by using an orthogonal transformation into a set of uncorrelated features, which are called principal components. After the PCA processing, some new features are created and the total number of features will be reduced. KPCA is developed as an extension of PCA by involving kernel methods for extracting nonlinear principal components [SCH 98]. This allows us to obtain new features with higher order correlations between original variables.

Factor analysis is similar to PCA which can be used to reduce dimensionality. It investigates whether a number of variables are linearly related to a lower number of unobservable variables (factors). The obtained interdependencies between original variables can be used to reduce the set of variables. Independent component analysis (ICA) is another feature extraction method. It is a powerful solution to the problem of blind signal separation. In this model, the original variables are linearly transformed into mixtures of some unknown latent variables which are statistically independent, so that these latent variables are called independent components of the original data. Different from PCA, which attempts to uncorrelate data, ICA aims at composing statistically independent features [LIU 99].

The above four methods have been used as data preprocessing methods for SVMs in various applications [CAO 03, QI 01, DÉN 03, FAR 09]. However, they are not the right choices for us. Our aim is to find the set of features which are not only optimal for learning algorithms, but also reachable in practice. It means that we need to select features from the original set without developing new features.

Some FS methods especially designed for SVMs have been proposed. Weston *et al.* [WES 00] reduced features by minimizing the radius-margin bound on the leave-one-out error via a gradient method. Fröhlic and Zell [FRÖ 04] incrementally chose features based on the regularized risk and a combination of backward elimination and exchange algorithm. Gold *et al.* [GOL 05] used a Bayesian approach, automatic relevance determination (ARD), to select relevant features. In [MAN 07], Mangasarian and Wild proposed a mixed-integer algorithm which was considered to be straightforward and easily implementable. All of these methods focus on eliminating irrelevant features or improving generalization ability. However, they do not consider the feasibility of selected features in a specific application domain, such as predicting energy consumption. Furthermore, they were implemented only for classification problems.

To the best of our knowledge, there is little work concerning FS of building energy consumption with regard to machine-learning methods. Most of the existing work derives models based on previously established sets of features. Madsen *et al.* [MAD 95] derived their continuous-time models on five variables, which are room air temperature, surface temperature, ambient dry bulb temperature, energy input from the electrical heaters and solar radiation on southern surface. Neto *et al.* [NET 08] built their neural network based on the input of daily average values of dry bulb temperature, relative humidity, global solar radiation and diffuse solar radiation. Azadeh *et al.* [AZA 08] and Maia *et al.* [MAI 09] forecast electrical energy consumption through analyzing the varying inner targets without any contributory variable involved. Yokoyama *et al.* [YOK 09] considered only two features, air temperature and relative humidity in their neural network model. Tso *et al.* [TSO 07] used more than 15 features in their assessment of traditional regression analysis, decision tree and neural networks. Similar approaches can be found in [DON 05a, BEN 04, WON 10] and [LAI 08].

5.3.2. *Algorithm*

FS aims at selecting the most useful feature set to establish a good predictor for the concerned learning algorithm. The irrelevant and unimportant features are discarded in order to reduce the dimensionality. Several advantages will be achieved if we wisely select the best subset of features. The first is the simplification of the calculation while keeping the dimensionality minimized, which could contribute to avoiding the problem of dimensionality curse. The second is the possible improvement of accuracy of the developed model. The third is the improved interpretability of the models. The last is the feasibility of obtaining accurate feature samples, especially for some time series problems in practice.

Two FS methods will be used in our approach to preprocess raw data before model training. The first one ranks the features individually by correlation coefficient between each feature and the target. We use CC to stand for this method. The correlation coefficient between two vectors X and Y of size N is defined as:

$$\text{Correlation}(f) = \frac{N \sum XY - (\sum X)(\sum Y)}{\sqrt{[N \sum X^2 - (\sum X)^2][N \sum Y^2 - (\sum Y)^2]}}$$

The other method is called regression gradient guided feature selection (RGS), which is developed by Navot *et al.* in the application of brain neural activities [NAV 06b]. We chose this method since it is designed especially for regression and has shown competitive ability to handle a complicated dependency of the target function on groups of features. The basic idea is to assign a weight to each feature and evaluate the weight vectors of all the features simultaneously by gradient ascent. The nonlinear function K-Nearest-Neighbor (KNN) is applied as the predictor to evaluate the dependency of the target on the features. The estimated target of sample x under KNN is defined as:

$$\hat{f}_w(x) = \frac{1}{Z} \sum_{x' \in N(x)} f(x') e^{-d(x,x')/\beta}$$

where $N(x)$ is the set of K nearest neighbors of sample x. Quantity

$$d(x, x') = \sum_{i=1}^{n} (x'_i - x_i)^2 w_i^2$$

is the distance between sample x and one of its nearest neighbors x', n is the number of features, w is the weight vector and w_i is the specific weight assigned to the ith feature. Quantity

$$Z = \sum_{x' \in N(x)} e^{-d(x',x)/\beta}$$

is a normalization factor and β is a Gaussian decay factor. Then, the optimal w can be found by maximizing the following evaluation function:

$$e(w) = -\frac{1}{2} \sum_{x \in S} (f(x) - \hat{f}_w(x))^2$$

where S is the sample for model training. Since $e(w)$ is smooth almost everywhere in a continuous domain, we can solve the extremum seeking problem by gradient ascent method. More details can be found in [NAV 06b].

5.3.3. *Feature set description*

We use the data generated in Chapter 2. For a single building, the hourly electric demands, together with hourly profiles of 23 features, are recorded through 1 year. Table 5.1 shows the recorded features and their units. It is known that building structures such as room space, wall thickness and windows area play important roles in the total energy consumption of a building. However, for one particular building, these variables have constant values through the simulation period, which means they do not contribute to SVR model learning. Therefore, it is practical to discard these variables in this set without losing accuracy in the model. Later, in the data of multiple buildings, we will take these factors into consideration. Concerning the data analyzing process, the data for model training are the first 10 months of 1 year's consumption (from January 1 to October 31) and for model testing are the remaining 2 months (from November 1 to December 31).

Since people do not usually work at weekends and holidays, the energy requirement on these days is quite low, compared to normal working days. This means weekends and holidays have totally different energy behaviors from working days. Take the 56th day as an example, it is a Saturday, the energy consumption for that day is 0.18, compared to other working days which have a normal consumption of more than 4, it can thus be safely ignored. It is proved that if we distinguish these two types of days, when training the model by predictive models such as neural networks, considerable performance improvements could be achieved [KAR 06, YAN 05]. Therefore, to simplify the model in our practice, we only select the consumption data of working days for use in model training and testing. Consequently, the number of samples for training is 5,064 and for testing is 1,008.

Features	Unit
Outdoor Dry Bulb	C
Outdoor Relative Humidity	$\%$
Wind Speed	m/s
Direct Solar	W/m^2
Ground Temperature	C
Outdoor Air Density	kg/m^3
Water Mains Temperature	C
Zone Total Internal Total Heat Gain	J
People Number Of Occupants	-
People Total Heat Gain	J
Lights Total Heat Gain	J
Electric Equipment Total Heat Gain	J
Window Heat Gain for each wall	W
Window Heat Loss for each wall	W
Zone Mean Air Temperature	C
Zone Infiltration Volume	m^3
District Heating Outlet Temp	C

Table 5.1. *Twenty-three features for the model training and testing on one building's consumption*

5.4. Model reduction for single building energy

5.4.1. *Feature set selection*

In this section, we experimentally analyze our approach to select the best subset of features for training statistical models on building energy consumption data. Since the number of features does not have a significant effect on the computational cost of SVM training, we put our focus primarily on the following two aspects, which are also two evaluation criteria of our method. The first is that the selected features should be potentially the most important ones to the predictor. In other words, the model generalization error should still be acceptable after FS. For this purpose, we have to involve some

FS algorithms in the object and choose the features with the highest rankings or scores. The second is to make sure that the selected features can be easily obtained in practice. Concerning the energy data, the values of the chosen features for each observation can normally be collected from measurements, surveys, related documents like building plans and so on. However, in practice, efficient and accurate data are difficult to obtain, therefore, reducing necessary features is always welcome.

The two methods RGS and CC described in section 5.3 are applied to evaluate the usefulness of features. The object dataset is the previous consumption of working days. The scores for each feature are listed in Table 5.2 in columns two and three. We can see that even the same feature could probably have totally different scores under the evaluation of two FS algorithms. For example, the outdoor dry bulb temperature is the most important feature under the judgment of RGS, while on the contrary, it is almost useless according to CC ranking method. As experimental results have shown, the features with the highest scores under RGS are generally more useful than those with the highest ranks according to CC. This indicates that RGS method is more applicable to SVR than CC method. However, since the feature subsets with low scores are possibly still useful for the learning algorithms [GUY 03], we take both RGS and CC into consideration while choosing the features.

The weather data can be recorded on site or gathered from meteorological department. We keep two weather features that have the highest scores under RGS, which are dry bulb temperature and outdoor air density. And at the same time, we discard relative humidity, wind speed, direct solar and ground temperature, no matter how their variations could contribute to energy requirement, as we naturally thought. The heat gain of the room consists of water mains' temperature, electrical equipment, and occupants' schedules. The part from the water mains' temperature corresponds to the water temperatures delivered by underground water main pipes. The part from electrical equipment such as lights and TVs, is determined by these equipments power. They could probably be measured or assessed in actual buildings. We divide the room into several zones according to their thermal dynamics. The two features, zone mean air temperature, which is the effective bulk air temperature of the zone, and zone infiltration volume which denotes hourly air infiltration of the zone, could also be measured or estimated in a normally operated building. All of the above selected features have scores not less than one. A special case we have to consider is the people number of occupants. This feature takes a middle place under RGS, but since it can be easily counted in real life and has a very high score under the evaluation of CC, we choose to keep it in the final subset. All other features will be discarded since they get low scores or are hard to collect in actual buildings. For example, zone total internal total heat gain is difficult to obtain directly and district heating outlet temp is useless according to CC. The selected features are indicated with stars in column Case I in Table 5.2.

Features	RGS	CC	Case I	Case II	Case III	Case IV	Case V
Outdoor Dry Bulb	1.61	0.29	*		*		*
Outdoor Relative Humidity	0.62	0.26			*	*	
Wind Speed	0.52	0.01			*	*	
Direct Solar	0.54	0.47				*	
Ground Temperature	0.99	0.07				*	
Outdoor Air Density	1.26	0.20	*				*
Water Mains Temperature	1.30	0.07	*				*
Zone Total Internal Total Heat Gain	1.01	0.67					
People Number Of Occupants	0.93	0.68	*	*	*		
People Total Heat Gain	0.93	0.68		*		*	
Lights Total Heat Gain	1.13	0.05	*		*		*
Electric Equipment Total Heat Gain	1.06	0.69	*	*	*		*
Window Heat Gain for each wall	1.03	0.62		*		*	
Window Heat Loss for each wall	0.93	0.50		*		*	
Window Heat Gain for each wall	0.82	0.35				*	
Window Heat Loss for each wall	0.82	0.49				*	
Window Heat Gain for each wall	0.73	0.56		*		*	
Window Heat Loss for each wall	0.82	0.48				*	
Window Heat Gain for each wall	0.89	0.56		*		*	
Window Heat Loss for each wall	0.95	0.50		*		*	
Zone Mean Air Temperature	1.14	0.22	*				*
Zone Infiltration Volume	1.00	0.34	*		*		
District Heating Outlet Temp	0.95	7.35e-4			*	*	

Table 5.2. *Scores of features evaluated by RGS and CC selection methods. The stars indicate selected features in that case.*

5.4.2. *Evaluation in experiments*

New datasets for both training and testing are generated by eliminating useless features from the datasets used in the previous experiment. Then, the model is retrained from the new training data and after applying the model to predict on the testing data, our results are as follows: MSE is $6.19 * 10^{-4}$ and

SCC is 0.97. To obtain a clear view of how the model performance changes before and after FS, we plot the measured and predicted daily consumptions in Figure 5.1. The relative errors are within the range $[-16\%, 12\%]$ as shown in Figure 5.2. We note that after FS, the number of features is 8, which is only one-third of the original set which has 23 features. However, compared to the results before FS, the model's prediction ability is still very high and the selected subset is, therefore, regarded as acceptable.

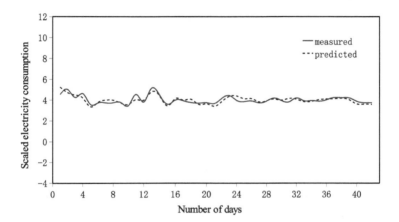

Figure 5.1. *Comparison of measured and predicted daily electricity consumption for a particular building on working days, with feature selection performed*

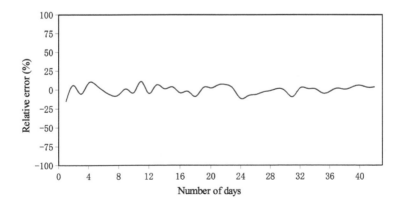

Figure 5.2. *Relative error for the prediction*

Four other subsets are formed in order to further evaluate if the selected feature set is optimal. They are indicated by columns Case II, Case III, Case IV and Case V in Table 5.2. In Case II, we select the top eight features under the evaluation of CC alone. By doing this, we are aiming at demonstrating whether the single CC is sufficient to select the best feature set. The zone total internal total heat gain feature is also ignored in this case just as we do in Case I. In Case III, we change three of the selected features to three other unselected ones. Outdoor air density, water mains temperature and zone mean air temperature, which are selected in Case I, are substituted with outdoor relative humidity, wind speed and district heating outlet temp. In Case IV, all of the selected features are substituted with other unselected ones except zone total internal total heat gain, which is not regarded as being directly obtainable in practice. In the last case, two features which gain the lowest scores are removed from the selected subset. They are number of occupants and zone infiltration volume.

Based on these considerations, four new datasets are generated both for training and testing, and a model is retrained for each case. We show the results of all five cases in Table 5.3. Two conclusions can be reached according to the results, the first one is that the designed FS method is valid due to model performance in Case I outperforming the other three cases. The other conclusion is that the SVR model with the RBF kernel has a stable performance since high-prediction accuracy is always achieved on all of the four subsets.

	Case I	Case II	Case III	Case IV	Case V
NF	8	8	8	14	6
MSE	6.2e-4	1.9e-3	7.5e-4	2.1e-3	9.2e-4
SCC	0.97	0.93	0.96	0.90	0.96

Table 5.3. *Comparison of model performance on different feature sets. NF: Number of features, MSE: Mean squared error, SCC: Squared correlation coefficient*

5.5. Model reduction for multiple buildings energy

Previously, we tested the FS method on one particular building's consumption over 1 year. In this section, we investigate how the subset of features influences the model performance on multiple buildings' consumption.

We choose the consumption data in the winter season for 50 buildings. The differences among these buildings mainly come from the weather conditions, building structures and the number of occupants. We suppose these buildings are randomly distributed across five cities in France: Paris-Orly, Marseilles, Strasbourg, Bordeaux and Lyon. As outlined in Figure 5.3, the five cities vary remarkably in ambient dry bulb temperatures, making the datasets represent energy requirements under five typical weather conditions. The buildings have diverse characteristics with randomly generated length, width, height and window/wall area ratio. The number of occupants is determined by the ground area and people density of the buildings. The time series data of those buildings are combined together to form the training sets. One more building is simulated for model evaluation purposes.

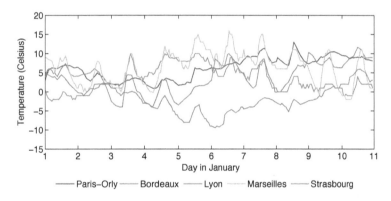

Figure 5.3. *Dry bulb temperature in the first 11 days of January. For a color version of the figure, www.iste.co.uk/magoules/mining.zip*

Two sets of consumption data are designed. The first set has 20 buildings and the second set includes all 50 buildings. To fully investigate how FS on these two datasets influences SVR models, two kernels are involved. In addition to the RBF kernel, we also test the performance of FS on SVR with a polynomial kernel, which is also applicable to nonlinear problems. The kernel parameter r is set to zero and d is estimated by fivefold cross-validation in a searching space $\{2, 3, ..., 7\}$. Selected features for representing multiple buildings are the feature sets for a single building plus building structures. Therefore, FS for multiple buildings has reduced the number of features from 28 to 12. The changes of MSE and SCC on these datasets are shown in Table 5.4. For clarification, the results of one single building are indicated in the same table.

			One building	20 buildings	50 buildings
RBF kernel	BF	MSE	4.8e-4	4.3e-4	4.4e-4
		SCC	0.97	0.97	0.97
	AF	MSE	6.2e-4	2.1e-3	3.7e-4
		SCC	0.97	0.96	0.97
Polynomial kernel	BF	MSE	8.0e-4	5.8e-4	5.9e-4
		SCC	0.96	0.96	0.96
	AF	MSE	2.1e-3	0.19	4.7e-4
		SCC	0.91	0.85	0.98

Table 5.4. *Prediction results of support vector regression with two kernel methods on three data sets. BF: Before feature selection, AF: After feature selection, MSE: Mean squared error, SCC: Squared correlation coefficient*

After FS, the accuracy of the prediction on 50 buildings' consumption improves significantly. With regard to 20 buildings' consumption, MSE increases to a certain extent, indicating a decrease in prediction accuracy. However, from the standpoint of SCC, the performance of the model with the RBF kernel involved is quite close to the situation without FS performed, as shown in Figure 5.4. With regard to the polynomial kernel, when training on the original datasets, the prediction ability of the model is just as good as RBF kernel, indicating that the polynomial kernel is also applicable on such a problem. After adopting FS, the performance of the model improves in the case of 50 buildings. Unfortunately, it decreases largely in the case of 20 buildings. It seems that the polynomial kernel is not as stable as RBF kernel when applied to such problems. However, we can see that it performs better for the case in 50 buildings than for that of 20 buildings. The same trend is also found for RBF kernel. These phenomena indicate that the proposed FS approach could give better performance to the models when more training samples are involved.

Another advantage of FS for statistical models is the reduction of training time. We show the time consumed for training SVR models with RBF kernel in Figure 5.5 where the time is in the logarithm form. The training time after FS is obviously less than that before FS, but the reduction is not too much. This phenomenon can be explained by the different parameter values we assigned for the learning algorithm, which always have a great influence on the training speed. We note that the time for choosing parameters for the predictor via cross-validation is too long to be ignored when evaluating a learning algorithm. While in this chapter we primarily focus on the influences of FS on predictors, the labor and time for choosing model parameters are not considered here since they are quite approximate before and after FS.

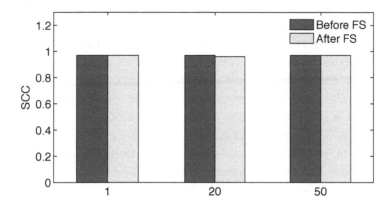

Figure 5.4. *Comparison of model performance from the standpoint of SCC before and after feature selection for radial basis function kernel*

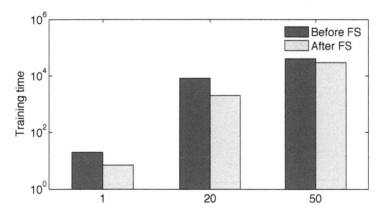

Figure 5.5. *Comparison of training time before and after FS for RBF kernel*

5.6. Concluding remarks

This chapter introduces a new feature selection method for applying support vector regression to predict the energy consumptions of office buildings.

To evaluate the proposed feature selection method, three datasets are first generated by EnergyPlus. They are time series consumptions for 1, 20 and 50 buildings, respectively. We assume that the developed models are applied to predict the energy requirements of actual buildings, therefore, the features are selected according to their feasibility in practice. To support the selection, we adopt two filter methods: the gradient-guided feature selection and the correlation coefficients, which can give each feature a score according to its usefulness to the predictor. Extensive experiments show that the selected subset is valid and can provide acceptable predictors. Performance improvement is achieved in some cases, e.g. accuracy remarkably enhanced for the models with either radial basis function or a polynomial kernel on 50 buildings' data, and the time for model learning decreases to a certain extent. We also identify that the performance improves when more training samples get involved. Besides radial basis function kernel, we proved that a polynomial kernel is also applicable to our application. However, it does not seem as stable as radial basis function kernel. Furthermore, it requires more complicated preprocessing work since more kernel parameters need to be estimated.

This preliminary work on feature selection for building energy consumptions has paved the way for its further progress. It serves as the first guide for selecting an optimal subset of features when applying machine-learning methods to the prediction of building energy consumption.

Parallel Computing for Support Vector Machines

6.1. Introduction

As introduced previously, the essential computation of SVMs is to solve a quadratic problem, which is both time and memory costly. This presents a challenge when solving large-scale problems. Despite several optimizing or heuristic methods such as shrinking, chunking [OSU 97], kernel caching [JOA 99], approximation of a kernel matrix [CHA 07], sequential minimal optimization (SMO) [PLA 99a] and a primal estimated subgradient solver [SHA 07], a more sophisticated and satisfactory resolution is always expected for this challenging problem. As stated previously, the building's energy system is extremely complex involving large number of influence factors, making tackling large-scale datasets common.

With the development of chip technologies, computers with multicores or multiprocessors are becoming more available and affordable in the modern market. This chapter, therefore, attempts to investigate and demonstrate how SVMs can benefit from this modern platform when solving the problem of predicting building energy consumption. A new parallel SVM that is particularly suitable to this platform is proposed. The decomposition method and inner SMO solver compose the main procedure of training. A shared cache is designed to store the kernel columns. For the purpose of achieving easy implementation without sacrificing performance, the new parallel programming framework MapReduce is chosen to perform the underlying parallelism. The proposed system is, therefore, called MRPsvm, abbreviation of MapReduce parallel SVM. We parallelize both classification and regression algorithms. Comparative experiments are conducted on five benchmarking datasets and three energy consumption datasets for SVC and SVR respectively, showing significant performance improvement in our system compared to the sequential implementation Libsvm [CHA 01] and the state-of-the-art parallel implementation Pisvm [BRU 07].

This chapter is organized as follows. Section 6.2 states the related work. Section 6.3 introduces the decomposition QP solver method for SVC. Section 6.5 explains some important issues with the MRPsvm's implementation. Section 6.5.4 presents numerical experiments on the performance test and comparative analysis based on benchmarking datasets. Section 6.6.1 uses the same mechanism to parallelize SVR and shows its application in predicting building energy consumption. Conclusions are drawn in section 6.7.

6.2. Overview of parallel support vector machines

Several approaches have been proposed to parallelize SVM, mostly for solving classification problems. They can be classified into several categories according to the type of QP solver.

Based on stochastic gradient descent method, P-packSVM optimizes SVM training directly on the primal form of SVM for arbitrary kernels [ZHU 09]. Very high efficiency and competitive accuracy have been achieved. Psvm proposed in [CHA 07] is based on an interior point QP solver. It approximates the kernel matrix by incomplete Cholesky factorization. Memory requirement is reduced and scalable performance has been achieved. Bickson *et al.* [BIC 08] solve the problem by Gaussian belief propagation which is a method from complex system domain. The parallel solver brings competitive speedup on large-scale problems. The decomposition method attracts more attention than the above solvers. Graf *et al.* [GRA 05] train several SVMs on small data partitions, then they aggregate support vectors from two-pair SVMs to form new training samples on which another training is performed. The aggregation is repeated until only one SVM remains. A similar idea is adopted by Dong *et al.* [DON 05b], in their work, sub-SVMs are performed on block diagonal matrices which are regarded as the approximation of the original kernel matrix. Consequently, non-support vectors are removed when dealing with these subproblems. Zanni *et al.* [ZAN 06] parallelize SVM-Light with improved working set selection and inner QP solver. Hazan *et al.* [HAZ 08] propose a parallel decomposition solver using Fenchel duality. Lu *et al.* [LU 08] parallelize randomized sampling algorithms for SVM and SVR. Cao *et al.* [CAO 06] and Catanzaro *et al.* [CAT 08] parallelize SMO solver for training SVM for classification. Both works mainly focus on updating gradient for KKT condition evaluation and the working set selection. The difference between them lies in the implementation details and the programming models. Specifically, the first work is conducted by using message passing interface (MPI) on clusters, while the second work is conducted by using MapReduce threads on modern GPU platform. In our work, we also adopt SMO algorithm. But, we use it as the inner QP solver without any parallel computation, in fact, we perform the parallelization on external decomposition procedure. The main advantage of our coarse-grained parallelism is that it can significantly reduce the burden of overheads since the number of iterations in global decomposition procedure (where $n \gg 2$) is much smaller than that of pure SMO algorithm (where $n = 2$). Although both GPU SVM [CAT 08] and our system are implemented in threads, we will not compare them in experiments since they are designed for different platforms and GPU SVM is especially used to solve classification problems.

6.3. Parallel quadratic problem solver

In section 3.3, we introduced interior point and gradient descent methods for QP solver. As we have stated, the third is the decomposition method. We present this approach in the following, and then based on it, we develop our parallel implementation.

The decomposition method reduces the problem into smaller tasks, then solves these small tasks and finally achieves global convergence. This method has attracted a lot of attention as the QP solver for SVMs in recent years, since it is quite efficient for large-scale problems and its memory requirement is also much less. It was first proposed by Osuna *et al.* to decompose the dual problem of SVMs [OSU 97]. In each small task, a working set which contains certain parts of α is selected to be optimized, while the rest of α remains at a constant value. The program repeats the select-optimize process iteratively until global optimality conditions are satisfied. In each iteration, only the involved partition of the kernel matrix needs to stay in the memory.

Similar to the dual form of SVC defined equation [3.17], we can write the general dual form of SVMs as:

$$\min_{\alpha} \ \frac{1}{2}\alpha^T Q\alpha - p\alpha \qquad [6.1]$$

under the constraints $\quad y^T\alpha = 0, \quad 0 \le \alpha \le C$

Let B denote the working set which has n variables and N denote the non-working set which has $(l - n)$ variables. Then, α, y, Q and p can be correspondingly written as:

$$\alpha = \begin{vmatrix} \alpha_B \\ \alpha_N \end{vmatrix}, \quad y = \begin{vmatrix} y_B \\ y_N \end{vmatrix}, \quad Q = \begin{vmatrix} Q_{BB} & Q_{BN} \\ Q_{NB} & Q_{NN} \end{vmatrix}, \quad p = \begin{vmatrix} p_B \\ p_N \end{vmatrix}$$

Accordingly, the small task of the dual form in this case can be written as:

$$\min \ \frac{1}{2}\alpha_B^T Q_{BB}\alpha_B - \alpha_B^T(p_B - Q_{BN}\alpha_N)$$

$$+ \frac{1}{2}\alpha_N^T Q_{NN}\alpha_N - \alpha_N^T p_N \qquad [6.2]$$

under the constraints

$$\alpha_B^T y_B + \alpha_N^T y_N = 0 \qquad [6.3]$$

$$0 \le \alpha_B \le C \qquad [6.4]$$

Since the last term $(\frac{1}{2}\alpha_N^T Q_{NN}\alpha_N - \alpha_N^T p_N)$ of equation [6.2] remains constant in each iteration, it can be omitted while calculating, so that minimization function [6.2] basically holds the same form as the original objective function [3.17]. One of the advantages of this decomposition method is that the newly generated task is small enough to be solved by most off-the-shelf methods, requiring less storage space, which is probably affordable for modern computers. To the extreme, if the working set contains only two variables each time, the derived algorithm is SMO. In fact, this is an efficient inner small task solver due to its relative simplicity, yet high-performance characteristics. This kind of binary subproblem can be easily solved analytically [PLA 99a, CHA 01]. As stated in [JOA 99], the solution of equation [6.2] is strictly feasible toward the optimum solution of global problem defined in equation [3.17]. This feature guarantees the global convergence of the decomposition method.

The KKT optimality conditions are verified through evaluating the gradient of [6.1], i.e.

$$f_i = \sum_{j=1}^{l} \alpha_j Q_{ij} + p_i \quad \text{for all} \quad i = 1, ..., l.$$

This procedure can be summarized as follows. First, we classify the training samples into two categories:

$$I_{up}(\alpha) = \{i | \alpha_i < C, y_i = 1 \text{ or } \alpha_i > 0, y_i = -1\}$$
$$I_{low}(\alpha) = \{i | \alpha_i < C, y_i = -1 \text{ or } \alpha_i > 0, y_i = 1\}$$

Then, we search two extreme values $m(\alpha)$ and $M(\alpha)$:

$$m(\alpha) = \max_{i \in I_{up}(\alpha)} - y_i f_i \qquad\qquad\qquad [6.5]$$

$$M(\alpha) = \min_{i \in I_{low}(\alpha)} - y_i f_i \qquad\qquad\qquad [6.6]$$

And finally, we define the stopping criterion as:

$$m(\alpha) - M(\alpha) \leq \epsilon \qquad\qquad\qquad [6.7]$$

The selection of working set directly influences the speed of convergence. For inner SMO solver, a maximal violating pair is selected to be the binary working set according to the first or second-order information [FAN 05]. We do not state here how inner SMO solver works since it has been discussed in detail in [PLA 99a] and [CHA 01].

For the selection of working set B, we simply consider the first-order information and select the maximal violating pairs, as proposed by Zanni

[ZAN 06]. Suppose the required size of B is n, we choose q $(q < n)$ variables from α by sequentially selecting pairs of variables which satisfy equations [6.5] and [6.6]. The remaining $(n - q)$ variables are chosen as those which entered B in the last iteration but have not yet been selected in current B. The selection of these $(n - q)$ variables follows the sequence: free variables $(0 < \alpha_i < C)$, lower bound variables $(\alpha_i = 0)$ and upper bound variables $(\alpha_i = C)$. The reason for putting restraint on the number of new variables entering the working set is to avoid frequent entering-leaving of certain variables. Otherwise, the speed of convergence would considerably slow down [ZAN 06].

After the working set is optimized, f is updated by the newly optimized $\alpha_j, \forall j \in B$. This procedure is crucial as it prepares f to do optimality condition evaluation and working set selection for the next iteration. In fact, this is the most computational expensive step in SVM training due to the heavy work of computing Q_{ij}. The updating procedure can be written as follows:

$$f_i^* = f_i + \sum_{j \in B} \Delta \alpha_j Q_{ij} \qquad i = 1, ..., l \qquad [6.8]$$

where $\Delta \alpha_j$ is the newly optimized α_j minus the old α_j. The whole decomposition method is summarized in algorithm 6.1.

Algorithm 6.1: *Decomposition solver of SVM*

Input: data set $(x_i, z_i), \forall i \in 1, ..., l$

Initialize: $\alpha_i = 0, y_i, f_i, \forall i \in 1, ..., l$

Calculate: $I_{up}, I_{low}, m(\alpha), M(\alpha)$

Repeat

    select working set B until $\mid B \mid = n$

    update α_i by SMO solver, $\forall i \in B$

    update $f_i, \forall i \in 1, ..., l$

    calculate $I_{up}, I_{low}, m(\alpha), M(\alpha)$

Until $m(\alpha) - M(\alpha) \leq \epsilon$

6.4. MPI-based parallel support vector machines

6.4.1. *Message passing interface programming model*

MPIis a library specification for message-passing parallel computation. Basically, processors have separate address spaces and the communication between processors is by sending and receiving message. MPI is mainly designed for distributed memory parallel architecture, in which each process is run on a separate node and communication is over high- performance switch. The rich libraries make it applicable to parallel computers, clusters and heterogeneous networks. However, it also supports shared memory programming model in which multiple processes can read/write to the same memory space. Several free while well-tested and efficient implementations of MPI are available in the public domain, such as MPICH, LAM, IBM's MPI, etc. These fostered the development of a parallel software industry, and there encouraged development of portable and scalable large-scale parallel applications.

MPI functions require that we specify the type of data which is sent between processors. This is because these functions pass variables, not defined types. If the data type is a standard one, such as int, char, double, etc., you can use predefined MPI datatypes such as MPI_INT, MPI_CHAR, MPI_DOUBLE.

Here is an example in C that passes an array of ints and all the processors want to send their arrays to the root with MPI_Gather:

```
int array[100];
int root,total_p,*receive_array;

MPI_Comm_size(comm, &total_p);
receive_array=malloc(total_p*100*sizeof(*receive_array));
MPI_Gather(array, 100, MPI_INT, receive_array, 100, MPI_INT,
    root, comm);
```

However, we may instead wish to send data as one block as opposed to 100 ints. To do this define a "contiguous block" derived data type.

```
MPI_Datatype newtype;
MPI_Type_contiguous(100, MPI_INT, &newtype);
MPI_Type_commit(&newtype);
MPI_Gather(array, 1, newtype, rec_array, 1, newtype, root,
    comm);
```

Passing a class or a data structure cannot use a predefined data type. MPI_Type_create_struct creates an MPI derived data type from MPI_predefined data types, as follows:

```
int MPI_Type_create_struct(int count, int blocklen[],
    MPI_Aint disp[], MPI_Datatype type[], MPI_Datatype *
    newtype)
```

where count is a number of blocks, also number of entries in blocklen, disp, and type. blocklen is the number of elements in each block (array of integer), disp is the byte displacement of each block (array of integer), type is the type of elements in each block (array of handles to datatype objects).

MPI uses objects called communicators and groups to define which collection of processes may communicate with each other. Most MPI routines require us to specify a communicator as an argument. Simply use MPI_COMM_WORLD whenever a communicator is required – it is the predefined communicator that includes all of our MPI processes.

Within a communicator, every process has its own unique, integer identifier assigned by the system when the process initializes. A rank is sometimes also called a task ID. Ranks are contiguous and begin at zero. Ranks are used by the programmer to specify the source and destination of messages, and are often used conditionally by the application to control program execution like in the expression (if rank=0 do this / if rank=1 do that).

Most MPI routines include a return/error code parameter, as described in the above functions. However, according to the MPI standard, the default behavior of an MPI call is to abort if there is an error. This means we will probably not be able to capture a return/error code other than MPI_SUCCESS (zero). The standard does provide a means to override this default error handler. The types of errors displayed to the user are implementation-dependent.

Most of the MPI point-to-point routines can be used in either blocking or non-blocking mode. In blocking mode, the send routine will only "return" after it is "safe" to modify the application buffer (your send data) for reuse. "Safe" means that modifications will not affect the data intended for the receive task. Safe does not imply that the data were actually received – it may very well be sitting in a system buffer. A blocking receive only "returns" after the data have arrived and are ready for use by the program.

While in non-blocking mode, the send and receive routines behave similarly – they will return almost immediately. They do not wait for any communication events to complete, such as message copying from user memory to system buffer space or the actual arrival of message. Non-blocking operations simply "request" the MPI library to perform the operation when it is able. The user cannot predict when that will happen. It is unsafe to modify the application buffer (our variable space) until we know for a fact the requested non-blocking operation was actually performed by the library. There are "wait" routines used to do this. Non-blocking communications are primarily used to overlap computation with communication and exploit possible performance gains.

In the next sections, we will introduce two parallel implementations of SVM, Pisvm and Psvm which are MPI-based implementation. We briefly introduce their features and advantages without going into implementation details. Indeed, since they are open source projects, readers can find their documents and codes on the Internet.

6.4.2. *Pisvm*

Pisvm is based on a decomposition method, allowing for efficient training and testing with various kernel functions. Its implementation is based on MPI. It is compatible with Libsvm, using the same input format and command line switches. It is a good substitute of the Libsvm when solving larger problems. It runs on any cluster computer where the MPI is available. It achieves superlinear speedups on some large-scale datasets. It supports training of all SVM formulations including C-SVC, ν-SVC for classification and ε-SVR, ν-SVR for regression.

Pisvm uses three different parallelization strategies for the interior point algorithm, the gradient projection algorithm and SMO in combination with the decomposition approach for SVM training. The gradient projection algorithm is successfully used for parallel C-SVC and its extension is explored to solve QP problems with two linear constraints that arise when training ν-SVC and ν-SVR. Unfortunately, this extension converges slowly, making it unapplicable in practice. Similar slow convergence is also found in parallel interior point implementation of the interior point algorithm. Therefore, parallel SMO is proposed and embraced in Pisvm.

This parallel implementation achieves superlinear speedups for C-SVC and ν-SVR. In the regression setting, Pisvm showed close to linear speedup on the Kddcup99 dataset benchmark, as explained later.

6.4.3. *Psvm*

Psvm tries to reduce memory use and parallelize both data loading and computation. The key step of PSVM is parallel incomplete Cholesky factorization (ICF). Traditional column-based ICF can reduce computational cost, but the initial memory requirement is higher. Psvm devises parallel row-based ICF as its initial step, which loads training instances onto parallel machines and performs factorization simultaneously on these machines. Once PICF has loaded n training data distributed on m machines, and reduced the size of the kernel matrix through factorization, interior-point method can be solved on parallel machines simultaneously.

Psvm first loads the training data in a round-robin manner onto m machines. Then, it performs a parallel row-based ICF on the loaded data. At the end of parallel ICF, each machine stores only a fraction of the factorized matrix. It then performs parallel interior point method to solve the quadratic optimization problem. The computation time is improved compared to the sequential and traditional parallel SVM implementations. However, linear speedup cannot be achieved when the number of machines continues to increase beyond a data-size-dependent threshold.

6.5. MapReduce-based parallel support vector machines

This section discusses some important issues with MRPsvm [PAN 12] implementation. The underlying parallelism is based on MapReduce framework. The communication and data decomposition is especially designed for multicore and multiprocessor systems.

6.5.1. *MapReduce programming model*

MapReduce is a new parallel programming framework originally proposed in [DEA 08] in Google. It allows users to write code in a functional style: map computations on separated data, generate intermediate key-value pairs and then reduce the summation of intermediate values assigned to the same key. A runtime system is designed to automatically handle low-level mapping, scheduling, parallel processing and fault tolerance. It is a simple, yet very useful framework, helping people extract parallelism of computations on large datasets by taking advantage of distributed systems as illustrated in [PAN 12, PAN 10]   and [PAN 13]. The Map and Reduce functions are defined with respect to data structured in key-value pairs.

Map function takes one pair of data with a type in one data domain, and returns a list of pairs in a different domain:

$$Map(k_1, v_1) \rightarrow list(k_2, v_2)$$

The Map function is applied in parallel to every item in the input dataset. This produces a list of (k_2, v_2) pairs for each call. After this, the MapReduce framework collects all pairs with the same key from all lists and groups them together, thus creating one group for each one of the different generated keys.

The Reduce function is then applied in parallel to each group, which in turn produces a collection of values in the same domain:

$$Reduce(k_2, list(v_2)) \rightarrow list(v_3)$$

Each Reduce call typically produces either one value v_3 or an empty return, though one call is allowed to return more than one value. The returns of all calls are collected as the desired result list. Reduce invocations are distributed by partitioning the intermediate key space into R pieces using a partitioning function, for instance: $hash(key)modR$. The number of partitions, i.e. R, and the partitioning function are specified by the user.

Thus, the MapReduce framework transforms a list of key-value pairs into a list of values. This behavior is different from the typical functional Data

Mining and Machine Learning in Building Energy Analysis programming map and reduce combination, which accepts a list of arbitrary values and returns one single value that combines all the values returned by Map.

It is necessary but not sufficient to have implementations of the map and reduce abstractions in order to implement MapReduce. Distributed implementations of MapReduce require a means of connecting the processes performing the Map and Reduce phases. This may be a distributed file system. Other options are possible, such as direct streaming from mappers to reducers, or for the mapping processors to serve up their results to reducers that query them.

Problem defined in equation [6.8] can be regarded as a summation of several computational expensive terms, as shown in the top right corner in Figure 6.1. Therefore, MapReduce is naturally suitable to deal with this problem. The working set B is uniformly decomposed into several small pieces, the calculation of f^* is also divided into several parts in the same manner as for B. Each part is then assigned to a mapper. After the parallel calculations of these mappers, final f^* is added up by the reducer. Here, j_k, $k = 1, ..., n$ is the variable index of working set in kernel matrix, which gives the kth variable in B with its index in Q as j_k. In practice, since some of $\Delta \alpha_i$ are so marginal that they can be omitted, it is not necessary to update f on all of the n variables.

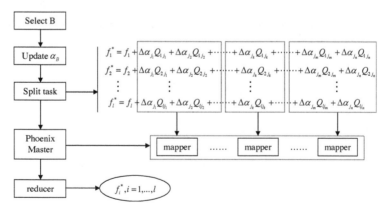

Figure 6.1. *Architecture of the parallelization in one iteration*

In some recent work, MapReduce has proved to be an effective parallel computing framework on multicore systems. Chu *et al.* [CHU 06] have developed MapReduce as a general programming framework on multicore systems for machine-learning applications. Phoenix designed in [RAN 07] implements a common API for MapReduce. It allows users to easily parallelize their applications without conducting concurrency management. The MapReduce tasks are performed in threads on multicore systems. An efficient integrated runtime system is supposed to handle the parallelization, resource management and fault recovery by itself. This system is adopted as the underlying MapReduce handler in our MRPsvm. We show the parallel architecture of one iteration in Figure 6.1. The small tasks are uniformly distributed to mappers which have the same number of processors. Phoenix serves as the role of creating and managing mappers and reducers, making the system easy to implement.

6.5.2. *Caching technique*

As stated in the previous sections, for large-scale problems, kernel matrix Q is too large to be stored in memory, and the calculation of kernel elements Q_{ij} is the dominant work that slows down the training. It is an effective technique to cache the kernel elements in memory as much as possible. MRPsvm maintains a fix-sized cache which stores recently accessed or generated kernel columns. The cache replacement policy is a simple least-recent-use strategy, the same as that of Libsvm. Only the column currently needed but not hit in the cache will be calculated. All parallel maps share unique copy of cache in the shared memory. In consequence, the operation of inserting a new column into the cache performed by whichever map should be synchronized.

For inner SMO solver, the kernel matrix size is dependent on the size of working set B which is normally set as 1,024 according to the knowledge gained by experience, it is practical to precompute and cache the full version of this small kernel matrix.

6.5.3. *Sparse data representation*

To reduce the storage requirements, the sample vectors x_i are stored in a sparse representation. When calculating a kernel column Q_{ij}, $i = 1, 2, ..., l$, we need to unroll the jth sample vector to dense format and then calculate the dot products of this vector with the other l sample vectors.

6.5.4. *Comparison of MRPsvm with Pisvm*

Pisvm also uses decomposition method to train SVM in parallel. It is an efficient tool to analyze multiple buildings' energy behaviors as stated in our previous work [ZHA 10]. However, its implementation is different from our new implementation MRPsvm in many aspects. First, Pisvm is based on MPI implementation and aims at extracting parallelism from distributed memory systems, while our parallel algorithm is conducted by MapReduce threads on shared memory system. The two implementations are based on totally different models. Second, in Pisvm, each process stores a copy of data samples, while on the contrary, MRPsvm stores only one copy in the shared memory. This means MRPsvm can save large amount of storage when the dataset is huge. The saved space can be used to cache more kernel matrix in order to further improve training speed. Third, Pisvm adopts a distributed cache strategy in order to share the saved kernel elements among all of the processes. Each process stores a piece of the cache locally. Consequently, the work for updating gradients is divided and assigned globally to proper processors according to the cache locality. In contrast, MRPsvm has only one copy of the cache, and each processor accesses the cache equally, so that the overhead of global assignment is avoided. However, we have to note that synchronization when writing in the cache is required.

In the next section, we will compare the performance of Pisvm with that of MRPsvm in real application datasets, providing direct evidence that our system is more efficient and suitable than the MPI implementation on multicore systems.

We test MRPsvm by comparing it with the parallel implementation Pisvm and the serial implementation Libsvm on five widely used benchmark datasets. Although this comparison may not be based on systems especially designed for multicore architecture, we still have good reasons for doing so. First, to the best of our knowledge, there is no existing parallel implementation of general SVM that is especially developed for multicore systems. Therefore, there is a strong need to verify if our system could outperform the state-of-the-art parallel implementation. Second, most of the systems surveyed in section 6.2 are not available to the public, while Pisvm, as a typical parallel implementation of SVM, is easy to obtain. Finally, the quadratic problem solver of Pisvm is the same as MRPsvm, hence, if we compare our system with Pisvm, the advantage of MapReduce framework is more convincing.

Two computers with different hardware architectures are adopted to check hardware effects. As shown in Table 6.2, the first computer has 4 cores with a shared L2 cache and memory. The second computer is a dual-processor system with 4 cores in each processor. The cores in the same processor share one cache, and the main memory is shared among all of the cores. Both of the two computers are running Linux 2.6.27-7.

Features	Computer I	Computer II
# of CPUs	1	2
# of cores	4	8
Frequency	1600MHz*4	2327MHz*8
Memory	2G	4G
L2 cache	4M	6M*2

Table 6.2. *Characteristics of the multi-core systems*

The five datasets are shown in Table 6.3. They vary in sample size and dimension. We train all SVMs with the Gaussian kernel. The tolerance of the termination criterion is set to 0.01. Since we focus on comparing three systems, the outputs of these classifiers may not be optimal. In other words, we do not guarantee that the parameters of SVM, i.e. C and γ, will reach optimal values. They are just chosen from the literature as shown in the last two lines of Table 6.3.

	Web	Adult	Mnist	Covtype	Kddcup99
# training samples	24,692	32,561	60,000	435,759	898,430
# testing samples	25,075	16,281	10,000	145,253	311,029
# Classes	2	2	2	8	2
# Dimensions	300	123	576	54	122
C	64	100	10	10	2
γ	7.8152	0.5	1.667	2e-5	0.6

Table 6.3. *Description of the five datasets and the two parameters of support vector machines on each dataset*

Since the caching technique is crucial for performance, for a reliable comparison, we set the cache size to be the same for all three systems. Furthermore, we restrict the cache size to be far smaller than the memory size in order to minimize page faults in runtime. Here, we have to emphasize that the following reported performance might not be optimal for all three systems, only serving for comparison purpose.

		Web	Adult	Mnist	Covtype	Kddcup99
Libsvm	Time	306.4	311.6	517.8	20260.7	726.8
	Accuracy	97.6%	82.7%	99.8%	51.0%	92.0%
Pisvm	Time	117.5	91.4	148.7	5612.6	415.5
	Accuracy	97.6%	82.7%	99.8%	51.0%	92.0%
	Speedup	2.6	3.4	3.5	3.6	1.7
MRPsvm	Time	65.8	59.2	123.2	3895.1	351.9
	Accuracy	97.6%	82.7%	99.8%	51.0%	92.0%
	Speedup	4.7	5.3	4.2	5.2	2.1

Table 6.4. *Training time and accuracy of the three systems on five datasets performed on computer I. The unit of time is second*

Table 6.7 shows the results of the three implementations performed on 4 processors. The time columns represent the whole training time, i.e. from reading the problem to writing the outputs. Here, we consider the speedup to denote how many times faster parallel implementation is over sequential implementation:

$$Speedup = \frac{Time\ of\ Libsvm}{Time\ of\ parallel\ implementation}$$

By analyzing the results, we can see that MRPsvm has successfully parallelized SVM training. For all five datasets, much more time is saved when running MRPsvm rather than Libsvm. Especially in the first four cases, the speed of MRPsvm is more than four times higher than that of Libsvm. In all of the cases, MRPsvm achieves outstandingly higher speedup than Pisvm, indicating that MRPsvm is more suitable than Pisvm on multicore systems.

We note that in these experiments, the accuracy of the three classifiers is almost the same. In fact, the numbers of support vectors generated by these classifiers are also quite close. In fact, these three implementations essentially have the same mechanism in quadratic problem solving, i.e. to iteratively optimize one pair of variables until achieving global optimization. The difference in runtime is mainly caused by the selected working set. Selecting different variables to perform optimization may induce totally different results in an iteration, but generally speaking, as long as global convergence is reached, the influence is marginal.

We show in Figure 6.2 the times up of the two parallel solvers over the sequential solver when running on the second computer. MRPsvm again outperforms Pisvm on all of the datasets. Among them, the best speedup is achieved on Adult, while the worst is found on Kddcup99. This indicates that MRPsvm performs better on smaller datasets. The main reasons for worse performance on larger problems are due to locality and overheads of reduction. In each map, the updating of f requires accessing the whole data samples and several temporal vectors with the size close to l. Therefore, for large datasets, it is difficult to guarantee the locality for using L2 cache, especially when the cache is shared by several threads. Since we partition the global problem in columns, each map generates l intermediate f_i, so that the reduction is costly when l is very large.

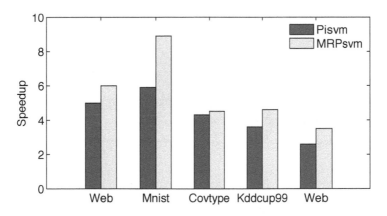

Figure 6.2. *Speedup of Pisvm and MRPsvm over Libsvm when running on computer II*

In fact, the parallel performance on 8 cores only slightly outperforms that on 4 cores. As explained at the beginning of this section, this is because we did not make full use of the memory on computer II. Far more time can be saved if we increase the cache size to the maximum with caution. In this optimal case, the cache size of MRPsvm and Libsvm is larger than that of Pisvm, since the former two systems generally require less memory. Therefore, this implies that more improvements can be achieved for MRPsvm and Libsvm than Pisvm.

6.6. MapReduce-based parallel ε-support vector regression

6.6.1. *Implementation aspects*

In this section, we use the same mechanism to parallelize SVR training process, and then apply this new parallel algorithm to predict building energy consumption. The above three implementations are compared again in this application.

First, we reformulate ε-SVR in the same form as the one defined in equation [6.1]. Let us present the training data as $(x_1, z_1), ..., (x_l, z_l)$, where vector x_i is the ith sample, z_i is the ith target value corresponding to x_i, l is the number of samples. The dual form of the SVR can be written in the following quadratic form:

$$\min_{\alpha} \quad \frac{1}{2}\alpha^T Q\alpha - \sum_{i=1}^{2l} p_i \alpha_i \qquad\qquad [6.9]$$

under the constraints $\quad y^T \alpha = 0$ [6.10]

$$0 \le \alpha_i \le C \quad \forall i = 1, ..., 2l \qquad\qquad [6.11]$$

where α is a vector of $2l$ variables, Q is a $2l$ by $2l$ kernel matrix. Each element of Q has the following form:

$$Q_{ij} = K(x_m, x_n)$$

$$m = \begin{cases} i & \text{if} \quad i \le l \\ i - l & \text{if} \quad i > l \end{cases}$$

$$n = \begin{cases} j & \text{if} \quad j \le l \\ j - l & \text{if} \quad j > l \end{cases}$$

$$i, j = 1, ..., 2l$$

where $K(x_i, x_j)$ is a kernel function. The parameter p in equation [6.9] is defined as:

$$p_i = \begin{cases} \varepsilon + z_i & \text{if} \quad i = 1, ..., l \\ \varepsilon - z_i & \text{if} \quad i = l+1, ..., 2l \end{cases} \qquad [6.12]$$

and the variable y in the constraint [6.10] is defined as:

$$y_i = \begin{cases} 1 & \text{if} \quad i = 1, ..., l \\ -1 & \text{if} \quad i = l+1, ..., 2l \end{cases} \qquad [6.13]$$

In the constraint [6.11], C is the upper bound used to trade off between model performance on training data and its generalization ability. The objective of the problem is to find the solution of α which minimizes equation [6.9] and fulfills constraint equations [6.10] and [6.11]. After the optimum α is found, the decision function can be formulated as:

$$g(x) = \sum_{i=1}^{l} (-\alpha_i + \alpha_{i+l}) K(x_i, x) + b$$

where only support vectors satisfy the relation: $-\alpha_i + \alpha_{i+l} \neq 0$.

6.6.2. *Energy consumption datasets*

Three datasets are prepared for the model training. They denote the historical energy consumption of one building, 20 buildings and 50 buildings, respectively. All of these buildings are located in urban areas. We evenly distribute them into five typical cities in France. The dry bulb temperatures of these five places is drawn in Figure 5.3. Each building has similar structures, i.e. single-story, mass-built, one rectangular room with an attic roof and four windows without shading. Electrical equipment including lighting systems, fans and water heaters, are scheduled as for common office use. In the winter season (from November 1 to March 31), district heating is applied in order to keep the room temperature at a constant level. Ventilation is adopted for indoor thermal comfort. The number of occupants depends on the housing space and people density, with the average of 0.2 people per zone floor area. During the simulation, some input variables such as size, orientation, window area and scheduling are set differently to achieve diversity among multiple buildings.

The dataset of one building is hourly energy dynamics in a period of 1 year. We select eight important features as shown in the Case I column in Table 5.2 according to the evaluation of our feature selection method. For two other datasets, the recording period is from November to March which is the winter season in France, and we record four more features which generate the building diversity, i.e. height, length, width and window/wall area ratio. Since weekends and holidays have totally different energy behaviors from working days, to simplify the model in our practice, we only use the consumption data of working days in the experiments. One more building is simulated for model evaluation purpose. The attributes of the three datasets are shown in Table 6.5.

Dataset	#tr	#te	Dimensions	C	γ	ε
One building	5064	1008	8	32	0.594	0.01
20 buildings	49940	2498	12	16	0.4193	0.01
50 buildings	124850	2498	12	16	0.4357	0.01

Table 6.5. *Description of the three datasets and the three parameters of support vector regression on each dataset. #tr: number of training samples, #te: number of testing samples*

6.6.3. *Evaluation for building energy prediction*

We perform the experiments on two shared memory systems as outlined in Table 6.6. To vary from the above computers, this time we use two different ones, the first has two cores while the second has four cores. Both of them have a shared L2 cache and memory and running 64 bit Linux system (kernel version 2.6.27-7). Their memory size is the same.

We train all SVRs with Gaussian kernel, the parameters as shown in the last three columns of Table 6.5. Again, we restrict the cache size to be far smaller than the memory size.

On each dataset, we train Libsvm, Pisvm and MRPsvm on both computer I and computer II. Table 6.7 shows the results of the three implementations performed on dual-core processor, including the number of support vectors (nSVs), MSE, SCC and training time. We show the training time on quad-core system in Table 6.8. Since nSVs, MSE and SCC in quad-core case are the same as those in dual-core case, we omit them in Table 6.8.

Features	Computer I	Computer II
# of CPUs	1	1
# of cores	2	4
Frequency	3.4GHz*2	1.6GHz*4
Memory	2G	2G
L2 cache	2M	4M

Table 6.6. *Characteristics of the experimental environment*

Data	Libsvm				Pisvm			
	nSVs	*MSE*	*SCC*	*Time*	*nSVs*	*MSE*	*SCC*	*Time*
1 bd	2150	6.16e-4	0.97	22.3	2162	6.10e-4	0.97	9.2
20 bd	9014	2.11e-3	0.96	3407.0	8967	2.12e-3	0.96	339.5
50 bd	22826	3.73e-4	0.97	44212.5	22823	3.74e-4	0.97	4179.8

Data	MRPsvm			
	nSVs	*MSE*	*SCC*	*Time*
1 bd	2168	6.14e-4	0.97	9.0
20 bd	8970	2.08e-3	0.96	212.7
50 bd	22799	3.73e-4	0.97	2745.8

Table 6.7. *Training time and performance of the three predictors on three datasets performed on computer I. bd: building, nSVs: number of support vectors, MSE: mean squared error, SCC: squared correlation coefficient. The unit of time is second*

We can see that, for all three datasets, the accuracy and the nSVs of MRPsvm are quite close to that of Libsvm and Pisvm. MRPsvm runs faster than Libsvm and Pisvm in all tests.

We show the speedup of MRPsvm and that of Pisvm comparatively in Figures 6.3, 6.4 and 6.5. For the case of one building, the speed of MRPsvm is twice as high as that of Libsvm. For the case of 20 and 50 buildings, MRPsvm performs more than 16 times faster than Libsvm. On both computers and on all three datasets, MRPsvm achieves remarkably higher speedup than Pisvm, indicating that MRPsvm is more suitable than Pisvm on multicore systems. The speed improvement by MRPsvm is particularly obvious in multiple building cases, indicating that MRPsvm performs better than Pisvm on much larger datasets. However, the better performance is not guaranteed on even larger problems due to locality and overheads of reduction as stated previously.

Dataset	Libsvm	Pisvm	MRPsvm
1 building	18.0	7.3	6.9
20 buildings	2532.1	214.1	133.5
50 buildings	32952.2	2325.5	1699.0

Table 6.8. *Training time of the three predictors performed on computer II. Time unit is second*

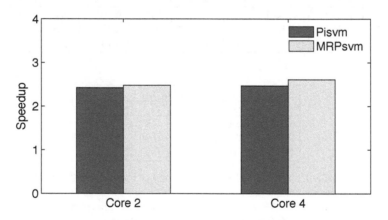

Figure 6.3. *Speedup of Pisvm and MRPsvm on one building's data*

6.7. Concluding remarks

This chapter proposes a parallel implementation of SVMs for multicore and multiprocessor systems. It implements the decomposition method and utilizes SMO as an inner solver. The parallelism is conducted to update the vector f in the decomposition step and is programmed in the simple, yet pragmatic programming framework MapReduce. A shared cache is designed to save the kernel matrix columns when the data size is very large. First, we use this mechanism to implement SVC, and the extensive experiments show that our system is very efficient in solving large-scale problems. For instance, the speed on 4 processors can increase to more than 4 times that of Libsvm for most of the applications. It overwhelms the state-of-the-art Pisvm in all benchmark tests in terms of both speed and memory requirement.

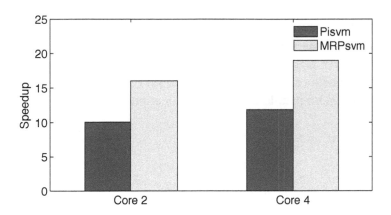

Figure 6.4. *Speedup of Pisvm and MRPsvm on 20 buildings' data*

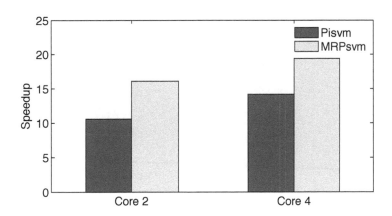

Figure 6.5. *Speedup of Pisvm and MRPsvm on 50 buildings' data*

We also parallelize SVR for solving large-scale problems in building energy analysis. Experimental results show that the new parallel system provides the same accuracy as Libsvm does, yet performs far more efficiently than the sequential implementation in solving stated problems. On the smallest dataset, MRPsvm achieves more than twice the speedup times of Libsvm while on the largest dataset, the speedup times can increase to 16-fold and 19-fold on dual-core system and on quad-core system, respectively. Again, the proposed implementation is superior to the Pisvm in all tests in terms of both speed and memory requirement.

Since the multicore system is dominating the trend of processor development and is highly available in the modern market, MRPsvm is potentially very practical and feasible in solving large-scale regression problems. Furthermore, the success of MRPsvm indicates that MapReduce is a suitable option for parallelizing machine-learning algorithms.

Summary and Future of Building Energy Analysis

The prediction of building energy consumption is an important task in building design, retrofit and operation. A well-designed building and its energy system may lead to energy conservation and CO_2 reduction. This book deals with up-to-date artificial intelligence models and optimization techniques related to this application.

Building energy consumption

In this book, we start with a review of recently developed models on predicting building energy consumption, including elaborate and simple engineering methods, statistical methods and artificial intelligence methods, especially ANNs and SVMs. This previous work includes solving all levels of energy analysis with appropriate models, optimizing model parameters, treating inputs for better performance, simplifying the problems and comparing different models. We then summarize the advantages and disadvantages of each model. Among existing methods, artificial intelligence models are attracting more and more attention in the research community.

Predicting building energy consumption

Then, this book attempts to apply SVMs in predicting building energy consumption. We present the SVM principles in depth, as well as some important extensions, including SVC, SVR, one-class SVM, multiclass SVM and transductive SVM. These models have demonstrated superiority in many sorts of applications due to ideas of maximum margin, regularization and the kernel method.

Before using SVMs in our application, we need to consider how to obtain historical consumption profiles. In this book, we choose to simulate them in EnergyPlus based on three considerations. First, sufficient and precise data are difficult to collect in reality. Second, our aim is to develop high-performance mathematical models instead of physical profiles of a building and its energy system. Third, EnergyPlus is a powerful simulation tool, and with calibration it can produce very precise building energy profiles, close to real energy consumption data. In our work, office buildings located in France are generated. We use real weather conditions as the inputs in order to make the simulated buildings more like real buildings. The diversity of multiple buildings comes from different structure characteristics, envelope materials, occupancy, etc.

As long as historical energy consumption data are recorded, SVR models are trained and tested on this prediction. Extensive experiments are designed to test the accuracy and robustness of this model by training on different types of historical data. Very high prediction accuracy is achieved. Generally speaking, the more are training data, the better is model performance. However, when the testing data have similar distribution with the training data, even small training datasets can derive high-performance models. For instance, the energy consumption in November is similar to that in January, and the model derived from January (1 month only) achieves better performance than the model derived from January–August (8 months). SVR also shows high accuracy in predicting a completely new building by involving building structure characteristics.

Detection and diagnosis of building energy faults

After predicting building energy consumption with SVR, in the next application, we use the RDP neural network model to detect and diagnose building energy faults. We simulate abnormal consumption by manually introducing performance degradation to electric devices. In the experiment, our RDP model shows very high detection ability. Then, we propose a new approach to point out the reasons for the faults. Our method is based on the evaluation of several RDP models, each of which is designed to be able to detect a particular equipment fault. These models are trained on historical faulty consumption, and the proposed method is able to sort the possible sources according to their possibilities of failure.

Feature selection and model reduction

A new feature selection method is also proposed for reducing the SVR input dimension. The features are selected according to their feasibility in practice and usefulness to the predictor. The last criterion is evaluated under two filter methods: the gradient guided feature selection and the correlation coefficients. To evaluate the proposed method, we use three training datasets to evaluate performance change in the model before and after feature selection. Experimental results show that the selected subset can provide competitive predictors. The number of features is reduced without losing model performance, making the model easier to use in practice. Performance improvement is achieved in some cases. For instance, with both RBF and polynomial kernel on the data from 50 buildings, the model accuracy increases and the learning cost decreases apparently. This work serves as the first guide for selecting an optimal subset of features when applying machine learning methods on the prediction of building energy consumption.

Parallel computing

When the training dataset is large, the SVM training process becomes costly and the storage requirement would be very high. For this reason, a new parallel approach is proposed to optimize the SVM training. It is based on a decomposition method where the variables are optimized iteratively. The parallelism is programmed in the simple, yet pragmatic programming framework MapReduce. A shared cache is designed to store kernel matrix columns. This implementation is specially suitable to multicore and multiprocessor systems, including GPU. We have tested both SVC and SVR in extensive experiments. The results show that our method is very efficient in solving large-scale problems. It achieves high speedup with regard to the sequential implementation. The results also show superior performance of our implementation over a state-of-the-art parallel implementation in both training speed and memory requirement.

Future work

As for the application of analyzing building energy consumption, there are still many research problems to address, including the establishment of databases collecting precise and sufficient historical consumption data from various cases for further research use. On these large-scale databases, it is then important to develop new and more effective, robust, reliable and efficient models. Artificial intelligence is undergoing fast development, and new ideas from this field might cause delightful result in energy analysis. Obviously, large-scale database will contain not only useful data for building energy analysis but it is also important to develop feature selection methods to reduce the number of parameters. Recent research in model reduction order has been carried out in the past few years. Extension of such approaches and development of new methods for energy data might improve the feature selection. Regarding the model optimization, one consideration is to further optimize the parallel SVM algorithm by shrinking; finding the best granularity of parallel work for a particular dataset.

Naturally, this book cannot provide a complete record of the many approaches, applications, features and methods related to building energy. However, it does give a review of the progress being made in addressing this issue. This book introduces new methods based on artificial intelligence to address both the prediction of energy consumption and the detection and diagnosis of building energy faults.

Bibliography

[ASH 02] ASHRAE Standards Committee, Guideline 14-2002, 2002.

[ALH 01] AL-HOMOUD M.S., "Computer-aided building energy analysis techniques", *Building and Environment*, vol. 36, no. 4, pp. 421–433, 2001.

[ANS 05] ANSARI F.A., MOKHTAR A.S., ABBAS K.A. *et al.*, "A simple approach for building cooling load estimation", *American Journal of Environmental Sciences*, vol. 1, no. 3, pp. 209–212, 2005.

[AYD 02] AYDINALP M., UGURSAL V.I., FUNG A.S., "Modeling of the appliance, lighting, and space-cooling energy consumptions in the residential sector using neural networks", *Applied Energy*, vol. 71, no. 2, pp. 87–110, 2002.

[AYD 04] AYDINALP M., UGURSAL V.I., FUNG A.S., "Modeling of the space and domestic hot-water heating energy-consumption in the residential sector using neural networks", *Applied Energy*, vol. 79, no. 2, pp. 159–178, 2004.

[AYD 08] AYDINALP-KOKSAL M., UGURSAL V.I., "Comparison of neural network, conditional demand analysis, and engineering approaches for modeling end-use energy consumption in the residential sector", *Applied Energy*, vol. 85, no. 4, pp. 271–296, 2008.

[AZA 08] AZADEH A., GHADERI S.F., SOHRABKHANI S., "Annual electricity consumption forecasting by neural network in high energy consuming industrial sectors", *Energy Conversion and Management*, vol. 49, no. 8, pp. 2272–2278, 2008.

[BAI 03] BAILEY M.B., KREIDER J.F., "Creating an automated chiller fault detection and diagnostics tool using a data fault library", *ISA Transactions*, vol. 42, no. 3, pp. 485–495, 2003.

[BAR 05a] BARLEY D., DERU M., PLESS S. *et al.*, Procedure for Measuring and Reporting Commercial Building Energy Performance. Report no. Report no. NREL/TP-550-38601, A national laboratory of the U.S. Department of Energy Office of Energy Efficiency & Renewable Energy, 2005.

[BAR 05b] BARNABY C.S., SPITLER J.D., "Development of the residential load factor method for heating and cooling load calculations", *ASHRAE Transactions*, vol. 111, no. 1, pp. 291–307, 2005.

[BAU 98] BAUER M., SCARTEZZINI J.L., "A simplified correlation method accounting for heating and cooling loads in energy-efficient buildings", *Energy and Buildings*, vol. 27, no. 2, pp. 147–154, 1998.

[BEN 02] BEN-NAKHI A.E., MAHMOUD M.A., "Energy conservation in buildings through efficient A/C control using neural networks", *Applied Energy*, vol. 73, no. 1, pp. 5–23, 2002.

[BEN 04] BEN-NAKHI A.E., MAHMOUD M.A., "Cooling load prediction for buildings using general regression neural networks", *Energy Conversion and Management*, vol. 45, nos.13–14, pp. 2127–2141, 2004.

[BEN 08] BEN-HUR A., ONG C.S., SONNENBURG S. *et al.*, "Support vector machines and kernels for computational biology", *PLoS Computational Biology*, vol. 4, no. 10, 2008.

[BI 03] BI J., BENNETT K., EMBRECHTS M. *et al.*, "Dimensionality reduction via sparse support vector machines", *Journal of Machine Learning Research*, vol. 3, pp. 1229–1243, 2003.

[BIC 08] BICKSON D., YOM-TOV E., DOLEV D., "A Gaussian belief propagation solver for large scale support vector machines", *Proceedings of the 5th European Conference on Complex Systems*, Jerusalem, Israel, 2008.

[BRU 07] BRUGGER D., "Parallel support vector machines", *Proceedings of the IFIP International Conference on Very Large Scale Integration of System on Chip*, 2007.

[CAO 03] CAO L.J., CHUA K.S., CHONG W.K. *et al.*, "A comparison of PCA, KPCA and ICA for dimensionality reduction in support vector machine", *Neurocomputing*, vol. 55, nos. 1–2, pp. 321–336, 2003.

[CAO 06] CAO L.J., KEERTHI S.S., ONG C.J. *et al.*, "Parallel sequential minimal optimization for the training of support vector machines", *IEEE Transactions on Nueral Networks*, vol. 17, no. 4, pp. 1039–1049, 2006.

[CAT 08] CATANZARO B., SUNDARAM N. *et al.*, "Fast support vector machine training and classification on graphics processors", *Proceedings of the 25th International Conference on Machine Learning*, pp. 104–111, 2008.

[CHA 01] CHANG C.C., LIN C.J., LIBSVM: a library for support vector machines, 2001, available at http://www.csie.ntu.edu.tw/cjlin/libsvm.

[CHA 07] CHANG E.Y., ZHU K., WANG H. *et al.*, "PSVM: parallelizing support vector machines on distributed computers", *NIPS*, available at http://code.google.com/p/psvm, vol. 20, 2007.

[CHI 01] CHIMACK M.J., "Determining baseline energy consumption and peak cooling loads of a 107-year-old science museum using DOE2.1E", *Proceedings of the Seventh International IBPSA Conference*, 2001.

[CHO 04] CHO S.-H., KIM W.-T., TAE C.-S. *et al.*, "Effect of length of measurement period on accuracy of predicted annual heating energy consumption of buildings", *Energy Conversion and Management*, vol. 45, nos. 18–19, pp. 2867–2878, 2004.

[CHO 05] CHO S.-H., YANG H.-C., ZAHEER-UDDIN M. *et al.*, "Transient pattern analysis for fault detection and diagnosis of HVAC systems", *Energy Conversion and Management*, vol. 46, nos. 18–19, pp. 3103–3116, 2005.

[CHU 06] CHU C.T., KIM S.K., LIN Y.A. *et al.*, BRADSKI G.R., NG A.Y., OLUKOTUN K., "Map-reduce for machine learning on multicore", *NIPS*, pp. 281–288, 2006.

[CLA 01] CLARKE J.A., *Energy Simulation in Building Design (2nd Edition)*, Butterworth-Heinemann, Oxford, 2001.

[COM 11] COMMISSARIAT GÉNÉRAL AU DÉVELOPPEMENT DURABLE, Bilan énergétique de la France pour 2010, 2011, available at www.statistiques.developpement-durable.gouv.fr.

[CRA 01] CRAWLEY D.B., LAWRIE L.K., WINKELMANN F.C. *et al.*, "EnergyPlus: creating a new-generation building energy simulation program", *Energy and Buildings*, vol. 33, no. 4, pp. 319–331, 2001.

[CRA 08] CRAWLEY D.B., HAND J.W., KUMMERT M. *et al.*, "Contrasting the capabilities of building energy performance simulation programs", *Building and Environment*, vol. 43, no. 4, pp. 661–673, 2008.

[DEA 08] DEAN J., GHEMAWAT S., "MapReduce: simplified data processing on large clusters", *Communications of the ACM*, vol. 51, no. 1, pp. 107–113, 2008.

[DÉN 03] DÉNIZ O., CASTRILLÓN M. *et al.*, "Face recognition using independent component analysis and support vector machines", *Pattern Recognition Letters*, vol. 24, pp. 2153–2157, 2003.

[DEX 01] DEXTER A.L., NGO D., "Fault diagnosis in air-conditioning systems: a multi-step fuzzy model-based approach", *HVAC&R Research*, vol. 7, no. 1, pp. 83–102, 2001.

[DHA 98] DHAR A., REDDY T.A., CLARIDGE D.E., "Modeling hourly energy use in commercial buildings with fourier series functional form", *ASME Journal of Solar Energy Engineering*, vol. 120, pp. 217–223, 1998.

[DHA 99] DHAR A., REDDY T.A., CLARIDGE D.E., "A Fourier series model to predict hourly heating and cooling energy use in commercial buildings with outdoor temperature as the only weather variable", *Journal of Solar Energy Engineering*, vol. 121, pp. 47–53, 1999.

[DIN 01] DING C.H.Q., DUBCHAK I., "Multi-class protein fold recognition using support vector machines and neural networks", *Bioinformatics/computer Applications in the Biosciences*, vol. 17, pp. 349–358, 2001.

[DON 05a] DONG B., CAO C., LEE S.E., "Applying support vector machines to predict building energy consumption in tropical region", *Energy and Buildings*, vol. 37, no. 5, pp. 545–553, 2005.

[DON 05b] DONG J.X., KRZYZAK A., SUEN C.Y., "Fast SVM training algorithm with decomposition on very large data sets", *IEEE Transactions on Pattern Analysis and Machine Intelligence*, vol. 27, no. 4, pp. 603–618, 2005.

[DOU 10] DOUNIS A.I., "Artificial intelligence for energy conservation in buildings", *Advances in Building Energy Research*, vol. 4, no. 1, pp. 267–299, 2010.

[DRU 96] DRUCKER H., BURGES C.J.C., KAUFMAN L. *et al.*, "Support vector regression machines,", *NIPS*, pp. 155–161, 1996.

[DU 10] DU J., ER M.J., RUTKOWSKI L., "Fault diagnosis of an air-handling unit system using a dynamic fuzzy-neural approach", *Proceedings of the 10th International Conference on Artificial Intelligence and Soft Computing: Part I*, ICAISC'10, Springer-Verlag, Berlin, Heidelberg, pp. pp. 58–65, 2010.

[DUA 03] DUAN K.-B., KEERTHI S.S., Which is the best multiclass SVM method? An empirical study, Report no. CD-03-12, Department of Mechanical Engineering, National University of Singapore, 2003.

[EKI 09] EKICI B.B., AKSOY U.T., "Prediction of building energy consumption by using artificial neural networks", *Advances in Engineering Software*, vol. 40, no. 5, pp. 356–362, 2009.

[ELI 06] ELIZONDO D., "The linear separability problem: some testing methods", *IEEE Transactions on Neural Networks*, vol. 17, no. 2, pp. 330–344, 2006.

[ELI 11] ELIZONDO D.A., DE LAZCANO-LOBATO J.M.O., BIRKENHEAD R., "Choice effect of linear separability testing methods on constructive neural network algorithms: an empirical study", *Expert Systems with Applications*, vol. 38, no. 3, pp. 2330–2346, 2011.

[ENE 11] EnergyPlus, 2011, available at http://www.EnergyPlus.gov.

[EUR 10] EUROPEAN PARLIAMENT AND COUNCIL, "Directive 2010/31/EU of the European Parliament and of the Council of 19 May 2010 on the energy performance of buildings", *Official Journal of the European Union*, vol. L153, pp. 13–35, 2010.

[FAN 05] FAN R.E., CHEN P.H., LIN C.J., "Working set selection using second order information for training support vector machines", *Journal of Machine Learning Research*, vol. 6, pp. 1889–1918, 2005.

[FAR 09] FARUQE M.O., HASAN M.A.M., "Face recognition using PCA and SVM", *Proceedings of the 3rd International Conference on Anti-Counterfeiting, Security, and Identification in Communication*, ASID'09, IEEE Press, Piscataway, NJ, pp. 97–101, 2009.

[FRI 96] FRIEDMAN J., *Another Approach to Polychotomous Classification*, Report, Department of Statistics, Stanford University, 1996.

[FRÖ 04] FRÖHLIC H., ZELL A., "Feature subset selection for support vector machines by incremental regularized risk minimization", *IEEE International Joint Conference on Neural Networks*, vol. 3, pp. 2041–2045, 2004.

[GHI 99] GHIAUS C., "Fault diagnosis of air conditioning systems based on qualitative bond graph", *Energy and Buildings*, vol. 30, no. 3, pp. 221–232, 1999.

[GHI 06] GHIAUS C., "Experimental estimation of building energy performance by robust regression", *Energy and Buildings*, vol. 38, no. 6, pp. 582–587, 2006.

[GOL 05] GOLD C., HOLUB A., SOLLICH P., "Bayesian approach to feature selection and parameter tuning for Support Vector Machine classifers", *Neural Networks*, vol. 18, nos. 5–6, pp. 693–701, 2005.

[GON 05] GONZÁLEZ P.A., ZAMARRENO J.M., "Prediction of hourly energy consumption in buildings based on a feedback artificial neural network", *Energy and Buildings*, vol. 37, no. 6, pp. 595–601, 2005.

[GOU 02] GOUDA M.M., DANAHER S., UNDERWOOD C.P., "Application of an artificial neural network for modelling the thermal dynamics of a building's space and its heating system", *Mathematical and Computer Modelling of Dynamical Systems: Methods, Tools and Applications in Engineering and Related Sciences*, vol. 8, no. 3, pp. 333–344, 2002.

[GRA 05] GRAF H.P., COSATTO E., BOTTOU L. *et al.*, "Parallel support vector machines: the cascade SVM", *Advances in Neural Information Processing Systems*, vol. 17, pp. 521–528, 2005.

[GUO 11] GUO J.J., WU J.Y., WANG R.Z., "A new approach to energy consumption prediction of domestic heat pump water heater based on grey system theory", *Energy and Buildings*, vol. 43, no. 6, pp. 1273–1279, 2011.

[GUY 03] GUYON I., ELISSEEFF A., "An introduction to variable and feature selection", *Journal of Machine Learning Research*, vol. 3, pp. 1157–1182, 2003.

[HAN 11] HAN H., GU B., WANG T. *et al.*, "Important sensors for chiller fault detection and diagnosis (FDD) from the perspective of feature selection and machine learning", *International Journal of Refrigeration*, vol. 34, no. 2, pp. 586–599, 2011.

[HAS 98] HASTIE T., TIBSHIRANI R., "Classification by pairwise coupling", *NIPS '97: Proceedings of the 1997 Conference on Advances in Neural Information Processing Systems 10*, MIT Press, Cambridge, MA,pp. 507–513, 1998.

[HAZ 08] HAZAN T., MAN A., SHASHUA A., "A parallel decomposition solver for SVM: distributed dual ascend using Fenchel duality", *IEEE Computer Society Conference on Computer Vision and Pattern Recognition*, pp. 1–8, 2008.

[HEE 12] HEEP: The Household Energy End-Use Project, 2012, available at http://www.branz.co.nz/HEEP.

[HOF 98] HOFFMAN A.J., "Peak demand control in commercial buildings with target peak adjustment based on load forecasting", *Proceedings of the IEEE International Conference on Control Applications*, vol. 2, pp. 1292–1296, 1998.

[HOU 99] HOUSE J.M., LEE W.Y., SHIN D.R., "Classification techniques for fault detection and diagnosis of an air handling unit", *ASHRAE Transactions*, pp. 1087–1097, 1999.

[HOU 06a] HOU Z., LIAN Z., YAO Y. *et al.*, "Cooling-load prediction by the combination of rough set theory and an artificial neural-network based on data-fusion technique", *Applied Energy*, vol. 83, no. 9, pp. 1033–1046, 2006.

[HOU 06b] HOU Z.J., LIAN Z.W., YAO H. *et al.*, "Data mining based sensor fault diagnosis and validation for building air conditioning system", *Energy Conversion and Management*, vol. 47, pp. 2479–2490, 2006.

[HOU 09] HOU Z., LIAN Z., "An application of support vector machines in cooling load prediction", *Proceedings of International Workshop on Intelligent Systems and Applications*, pp. 1–4, 2009.

[ISO 08] ISO 13790:2008, Energy performance of buildings – Calculation of energy use for space heating and cooling, ISO, Geneva, Switzerland, 2008.

[JAA 99] JAAKKOLA T., DIEKHANS M., HAUSSLER D., "Using the Fisher kernel method to detect remote protein homologies", *Intelligent Systems in Molecular Biology*, pp. 149–158, 1999.

[JAV 95] JAVEED NIZAMI S.S.A.K., AL-GARNI A.Z., "Forecasting electric energy consumption using neural networks", *Energy Policy*, vol. 23, no. 12, pp. 1097–1104, 1995.

[JIM 05] JIMÉNEZ M.J., HERAS M.R., "Application of multi-output ARX models for estimation of the U and g values of building components in outdoor testing", *Solar Energy*, vol. 79, no. 3, pp. 302–310, 2005.

[JOA 98] JOACHIMS T., "Text categorization with support vector machines: learning with many relevant features", in NÉDELLEC C., ROUVEIROL C., (eds), *Proceedings of ECML-98, 10th European Conference on Machine Learning*, vol. 1398, Springer Verlag, Heidelberg, pp. 137–142, 1998.

[JOA 99] JOACHIMS T., "Making large-scale support vector machine learning practical", *Advances in Kernel Methods: Support Vector Learning*, MIT Press, pp. 169–184, 1999.

[JOI 92] JOINT CENTER FOR ENERGY MANAGEMENT (JCEM), Final report: artificial neural networks applied to LoanSTAR data, Report no. TR/92/15, 1992.

[KAJ 96] KAJL S., POULIN R., MALINOWSKI P. *et al.*, "Fuzzy assistant for evaluation of building energy consumption", *Proceedings of International Fuzzy Systems and Intelligent Control Conference*, pp. 67–74, 1996.

[KAJ 97] KAJL S., ROBERGE M.A., LAMARCHE L. *et al.*, "Evaluation of building energy consumption based on fuzzy logic and neural networks applications", *Proc. of CLIMA 2000 Conference*, p. 264, 1997.

[KAL 97] KALOGIROU S.A., NEOCLEOUS C.C., SCHIZAS C.N., "Building heating load estimation using artificial neural networks", *Proceedings of the 17th International Conference on Parallel Architectures and Compilation Techniques*, 1997.

[KAL 00] KALOGIROU S.A., BOJIC M., "Artificial neural networks for the prediction of the energy consumption of a passive solar building", *Energy*, vol. 25, no. 5, pp. 479–491, 2000.

[KAL 06] KALOGIROU S.A., "Artificial neural networks in energy applications in buildings", *International Journal of Low-Carbon Technologies*, vol. 1, no. 3, pp. 201–216, 2006.

[KAR 06] KARATASOU S., SANTAMOURIS M., GEROS V., "Modeling and predicting building's energy use with artificial neural networks: Methods and results", *Energy and Buildings*, vol. 38, no. 8, pp. 949–958, 2006.

[KIM 95] KIMBARA A., KUROSU S., ENDO R. *et al.*, "On-line prediction for load profile of an air-conditioning system", *ASHRAE Transactions*, vol. 101, no. 2, pp. 198–207, 1995.

[KIM 05] KIM M., KIM M.S., "Performance investigation of a variable speed vapor compression system for fault detection and diagnosis", *International Journal of Refrigeration*, vol. 28, no. 4, pp. 481–488, 2005.

[KRA 03] KRARTI M., "An Overview of artificial intelligence-based methods for building energy systems", *Journal of Solar Energy Engineering*, vol. 125, no. 3, pp. 331–342, 2003.

[KRE 94] KREIDER J.F., HABERL J.S., "Predicting hourly building energy use: the great energy predictor shootout–overview and discussion of results", *ASHRAE Transactions*, vol. 100, pp. 1104–1118, 1994.

[KRE 95] KREIDER J.F., CLARIDGE D.E., CURTISS P., DODIER R. *et al.*, "Building energy use prediction and system identification using recurrent neural networks", *Journal of Solar Energy Engineering*, vol. 117, no. 3, pp. 161–166, 1995.

[KRE 99] KREBEL U.H.-G., *"Pairwise Classification and Support Vector Machines"*, MIT Press, Cambridge, MA, pp. 255–268, 1999.

[KUB 00] KUBOTA N., HASHIMOTO S., KOJIMA F. *et al.*, "GP-preprocessed fuzzy inference for the energy load prediction", *Proceedings of the 2000 Congress on Evolutionary Computation*, vol. 1, pp. 1–6, 2000.

[KUS 10] KUSIAK A., LI M., ZHANG Z., "A data-driven approach for steam load prediction in buildings", *Applied Energy*, vol. 87, no. 3, pp. 925–933, 2010.

[LAF 94] LAFRANCE G., PERRON D., "Evolution of residential electricity demand by end-use in Quebec 1979-1989: a conditional demand analysis", *Energy Studies Review*, vol. 6, no. 2, pp. 164–173, 1994.

[LAI 08] LAI F., MAGOULÈS F., LHERMINIER F., "Vapnik's learning theory applied to energy consumption forecasts in residential buildings", *International Journal of Computer Mathematics*, vol. 85, no. 10, pp. 1563–1588, 2008.

[LAM 10] LAM J.C., WAN K.K.W., WONG S.L. *et al.*, "Principal component analysis and long-term building energy simulation correlation", *Energy Conversion and Management*, vol. 51, no. 1, pp. 135–139, 2010.

[LEE 97] LEE W.Y., HOUSE J.M., SHIN D.R., "Fault diagnosis and temperature sensor recovery for an air-handling unit", *ASHRAE Transactions*, vol. 103, no. 1, pp. 621–633, 1997.

[LEE 04] LEE W.-Y., HOUSE J.M., KYONG N.-H., "Subsystem level fault diagnosis of a building's air-handling unit using general regression neural networks", *Applied Energy*, vol. 77, no. 2, pp. 153–170, 2004.

[LEI 09] LEI F., HU P., "A baseline model for office building energy consumption in hot summer and cold winter region", *Proceedings of International Conference on Management and Service Science*, pp. 1–4, 2009.

[LI 09] LI Q., MENG Q.L., CAI J.J. *et al.*, "Applying support vector machine to predict hourly cooling load in the building", *Applied Energy*, vol. 86, no. 10, pp. 2249–2256, 2009.

[LI 10a] LI Q., REN P., MENG Q., "Prediction model of annual energy consumption of residential buildings", *Proceedings of 2010 International Conference on Advances in Energy Engineering*, pp. 223–226, 2010.

[LI 10b] LI X., DENG Y., DING L. *et al.*, "Building cooling load forecasting using fuzzy support vector machine and fuzzy C-mean clustering", *Proceedings of International Conference on Computer and Communication Technologies in Agriculture Engineering*, pp. 438–441, 2010.

[LI 10c] LI X., DING L., LV J. *et al.*, "A novel hybrid approach of KPCA and SVM for building cooling load prediction", *Proceedings of 2010 Third International Conference on Knowledge Discovery and Data Mining*, pp. 522–526, 2010.

[LIA 03] LIAO L., NOBLE W.S., "Combining pairwise sequence similarity and support vector machines for detecting remote protein evolutionary and structural relationships", *Journal of Computational Biology*, vol. 10, no. 6, pp. 857–868, 2003.

[LIA 07] LIANG J., DU R., "Model-based fault detection and diagnosis of HVAC systems using support vector machine method", *International Journal of Refrigeration*, vol. 30, no. 6, pp. 1104–1114, 2007.

[LIU 99] LIU C., WECHSLER H., "Comparative assessment of independent component analysis (ICA) for face recognition", *International Conference on Audio and Video Based Biometric Person Authentication*, pp. 22–24, 1999.

[LIU 02] LIU M., SONG L., CLARIDGE D.E., "Development of whole-building fault detection methods", *High Performance Commerical Building Systems*, 2002.

[LOG 01] LOGAN B., MORENO P., SUZEK B. *et al.*, A Study of Remote Homology Detection, Report , Cambridge Research Laboratory, 2001.

[LU 08] LU Y., ROYCHOWDHURY V., "Parallel randomized sampling for support vector machine (SVM) and support vector regression (SVR)", *Knowledge and Information Systems*, vol. 14, pp. 233–247, 2008.

[LUN 02] LUNDIN M., ANDERSSON S., OSTIN R., "Validation of a neural network method for estimation heat loss and domestic gain in buildings", *Proceedings of the 6th Symposium on Building Physics in the Nordic Countries*, pp. 325–332, 2002.

[LUN 04] LUNDIN M., ANDERSSON S., ÖSTIN R., "Development and validation of a method aimed at estimating building performance parameters", *Energy and Buildings*, vol. 36, no. 9, pp. 905–914, 2004.

[LV 10] LV J., LI X., DING L. *et al.*, "Applying principal component analysis and weighted support vector machine in building cooling load forecasting", *Proceedings of International Conference on Computer and Communication Technologies in Agriculture Engineering*, pp. 434–437, 2010.

[MA 10] MA Y., YU J.-Q., YANG C.-Y. *et al.*, "Study on power energy consumption model for large-scale public building", *Proceedings of the 2nd International Workshop on Intelligent Systems and Applications*, pp. 1–4, 2010.

[MAD 95] MADSEN H., HOLST J., "Estimation of continuous-time models for the heat dynamics of a building", *Energy and Buildings*, vol. 22, no. 1, pp. 67–79, 1995.

[MAG 13] MAGOULÈS F., ZHAO H.-X., ELIZONDO D., "Development of an RDP neural network for building energy consumption fault detection diagnosis", *Energy and Buildings*, vol. 62, pp. 133–138, 2013.

[MAI 09] MAIA C.A., GONÇALVES M.M., "A methodology for short-term electric load forecasting based on specialized recursive digital filters", *Computers and Industrial Engineering*, vol. 57, no. 3, pp. 724–731, 2009.

[MAN 07] MANGASARIAN O.L., KOU G., "Feature selection for nonlinear kernel support vector machines", *Proceedings of the Seventh IEEE International Conference on Data Mining Workshops*, ICDMW'07, IEEE Computer Society, Washington, DC, pp. 231–236, 2007.

[MCQ 05] MCQUISTON F.C., PARKER J.D., SPITLER J.D., *Heating, Ventilating and Air Conditioning Analysis and Design*, 6th ed., Wiley, 2005.

[MEH 92] MEHROTRA S., "On the implementation of a primal-dual interior point method", *SIAM Journal on Optimization*, vol. 2, no. 4, pp. 575–601, 1992.

[NAM 07] NAMBURU S.M., AZAM M.S., LUO J. *et al.*, "Data-driven modeling, fault diagnosis and optimal sensor selection for HVAC chillers", *IEEE Transactions on Automation Science and Engineering*, vol. 4, pp. 469–473, 2007.

[NAV 06a] NAVARRO-ESBRI J., TORRELLA E., CABELLO R., "A vapour compression chiller fault detection technique based on adaptative algorithms. Application to on-line refrigerant leakage detection", *International Journal of Refrigeration*, vol. 29, no. 5, pp. 716–723, 2006.

[NAV 06b] NAVOT A., SHPIGELMAN L., TISHBY N. *et al.*, "Nearest neighbor based feature selection for regression and its application to neural activity", in WEISS Y., SCHOLKOPF B., PLATT J., (eds), *Advances in Neural Information Processing Systems 18*, MIT Press, pp. 995–1002, 2006.

[NET 08] NETO A.H., FIORELLI F.A.S., "Comparison between detailed model simulation and artificial neural network for forecasting building energy consumption", *Energy and Buildings*, vol. 40, no. 12, pp. 2169–2176, 2008.

[NEW 10] NEWSHAM G.R., BIRT B.J., "Building-level occupancy data to improve ARIMA-based electricity use forecasts", *Proceedings of the 2nd ACM Workshop on Embedded Sensing Systems for Energy-Efficiency in Building*, BuildSys '10, ACM, New York, NY, pp. 13–18, 2010.

[NOB 04] NOBLE W.S., "Support Vector Machine Applications in Computational Biology", *Computational Molecular Biology*, MIT Press, 2004.

[NOR 94] NORFORD L., SOCOLOW R., HSIEH E. *et al.*, "Two-to-one discrepancy between measured and predicted performance of a low-energy office building: insights from a reconciliation based on the DOE-2 model", *Energy and Buildings*, 1994.

[NOR 02] NORFORD L.K., WRIGHT J.A., BUSWELL R.A. *et al.*, "Demonstration of fault detection and diagnosis methods for air-handling units", *HVAC & R Research*, vol. 8, no. 1, pp. 41–77, 2002.

[OLO 98] OLOFSSON T., ANDERSSON S., ÖSTIN R., "A method for predicting the annual building heating demand based on limited performance data", *Energy and Buildings*, vol. 28, no. 1, pp. 101–108, 1998.

[OLO 99] OLOFSSON T., ANDERSSON S., "Analysis of the interaction between heating and domestic load in occupied single-family buildings", *Proceedings of the 5th Symposium on Building Physics in the Nordic Countries*, pp. 473–480, 1999.

[OLO 01] OLOFSSON T., ANDERSSON S., "Long-term energy demand predictions based on short-term measured data", *Energy and Buildings*, vol. 33, no. 2, pp. 85–91, 2001.

[OLO 02] OLOFSSON T., ANDERSSON S., "Overall heat loss coefficient and domestic energy gain factor for single-family buildings", *Building and Environment*, vol. 37, no. 11, pp. 1019–1026, 2002.

[OSU 97] OSUNA E., FREUND R., GIROSI F., "Training support vector machines: an application to face detection", *Proceedings of the Conference on Computer Vision and Pattern Recognition*, pp. 130–136, 1997.

[PAN 07] PAN Y., HUANG Z., WU G., "Calibrated building energy simulation and its application in a high-rise commercial building in Shanghai", *Energy and Buildings*, vol. 39, no. 6, pp. 651–657, 2007.

[PAN 10] PAN J., MAGOULÈS F., BIANNIC Y.L., "Implementing and optimizing multiple group-by query in a MapReduce approach", *Journal of Algorithms and Computational Technology*, vol. 4, no. 2, pp. 183–206, 2010.

[PAN 12] PAN J., MAGOULÈS F., BIANNIC Y.L., "MapReduce-based parallel algorithms for multidimensionnal data analysis", *Journal of Algorithms and Computational Technology*, vol. 6, no. 2, pp. 325–350, 2012.

[PAN 13] PAN J., MAGOULÈS F., BIANNIC Y.L. *et al.*, "Parallelizing multiple group-by queries using MapReduce: optimization and cost estimation", *Telecommunication Systems*, vol. 52, no. 2, pp. 635–645, 2013.

[PED 02] PEDRINI A., WESTPHAL F., LAMBERTS R., "A methodology for building energy modelling and calibration in warm climates", *Building and Environment*, vol. 37, nos. 8–9, pp. 903–912, 2002.

[PFA 05] PFAFFEROTT J., HERKEL S., WAPLER J., "Thermal building behaviour in summer: long-term data evaluation using simplified models", *Energy and Buildings*, vol. 37, no. 8, pp. 844–852, 2005.

[PLA 99a] PLATT J.C., "Fast training of support vector machines using sequential minimal optimization", *Advances in Kernel Methods: Support Vector Learning*, MIT Press, pp. 185–208, 1999.

[PLA 99b] PLATT J.C., "Probabilistic outputs for support vector machines and comparisons to regularized likelihood methods", *Advances in Large Margin Classifiers*, MIT Press, pp. 61–74, 1999.

[QI 01] QI Y., DOERMANN D., DEMENTHON D., "Hybrid independent component analysis and support vector machine learning scheme for face detection", *International Conference on Acoustics, Speech, and Signal Processing*, 2001.

[QIN 05] QIN J., WANG S., "A fault detection and diagnosis strategy of VAV air-conditioning systems for improved energy and control performances", *Energy and Buildings*, vol. 37, no. 10, pp. 1035–1048, 2005.

[RAN 07] RANGER C., RAGHURAMAN R., PENMETSA A. *et al.*, "Evaluating MapReduce for multi-core and multiprocessor systems", *Proceedings of the IEEE 13th International Symposium on High Performance Computer Architecture*, pp. 13–24, 2007.

[RED 06] REDDY A., "Literature review on calibration of building energy simulation programs: uses, problems, procedures, uncertainty, and tools", *ASHRAE Transactions*, vol. 112, no. 2, pp. 226–240, 2006.

[REE 99] REED R.D., MARKS II R.J., *Neural Smithing: Supervised Learning in Feedforward Artificial Neural Networks (Bradford Book)*, MIT Press, 1999.

[RIC 10] RICE A., HAY S., RYDER-COOK D., "A limited-data model of building energy consumption", *Proceedings of the 2nd ACM Workshop on Embedded Sensing Systems for Energy-Efficiency in Buildings*, pp. 67–72, 2010.

[ROS 01] ROSIPAL R., GIROLAMI M., TREJO L.J., "Kernel PCA for feature extraction and de-noising in non-linear regression", *Neural Computing & Applications*, vol. 10, pp. 231–243, 2001.

[ROT 01] ROTH V., "Probabilistic Discriminative Kernel Classifiers for Multi-class Problems", *DAGM Symposium Symposium for Pattern Recognition*, pp. 246-253, 2001.

[SCH 98] SCHÖLKOPF B., SMOLA A., MÜLLER K.-R., "Nonlinear component analysis as a kernel eigenvalue problem", *Neural Computation*, vol. 10, pp. 1299–1319, 1998.

[SCH 00] SCHÖLKOPF B., SMOLA A.J. *et al.*, "New support vector algorithms", *Neural Computation*, vol. 12, pp. 1207–1245, 2000.

[SCH 01] SCHÖLKOPF B., PLATT J.C., SHAWE-TAYLOR J.C. *et al.*, "Estimating the support of a high-dimensional distribution", *Neural Computation*, vol. 13, pp. 1443–1471, 2001.

[SCH 02] SCHÖLKOPF B., S.A.J., *Learning with Kernels: Support Vector Machines, Regularization, Optimization, and Beyond*, MIT Press, 2002.

[SCH 06] SCHEIN J., BUSHBY S.T., CASTRO N.S. *et al.*, "A rule-based fault detection method for air handling units", *Energy and Buildings*, vol. 38, no. 12, pp. 1485–1492, 2006.

[SEB 02] SEBASTIANI F., RICERCHE C.N.D., "Machine learning in automated text categorization", *ACM Computing Surveys*, vol. 34, pp. 1–47, 2002.

[SHA 07] SHALEV-SHWARTZ S., SINGER Y., SREBRO N., "Pegasos: primal estimated sub-GrAdient SOlver for SVM", *Proceedings of the 24th International Conference on Machine Learning*, pp. 807–814, 2007.

[SHA 08] SHALEV-SHWARTZ S., SREBRO N., "SVM optimization: inverse dependence on training set size", *Communications*, pp. 928–935, 2008.

[SIM 11] "Building Energy Software Tools Directory", 2011, available at http://apps1.eere.energy.gov/buildings/tools_directory/ (Accessed March 2011).

[SON 03] SONG L., LIU M., CLARIDGE D.E. *et al.*, "Study of on-line simulation for whole building level energy consumption fault detection and optimization", *Proceedings of Architectural Engineering: Building Integration Solutions*, Austin, TX, pp. 76–83, 2003.

[SON 08] HAK SONG Y., AKASHI Y., YEE J.-J., "A development of easy-to-use tool for fault detection and diagnosis in building air-conditioning systems", *Energy and Buildings*, vol. 40, no. 2, pp. 71–82, 2008.

[SVM 11] SVM software, 2011, available at http://www.support-vector-machines.org/SVMsoft.html.

[TAJ 98a] TAJINE M., ELIZONDO D., "Growing methods for constructing recursive deterministic perceptron neural networks and knowledge extraction", *Artificial Intelligence*, vol. 102, no. 2, pp. 295–322, 1998.

[TAJ 98b] TAJINE M., ELIZONDO D., "The recursive deterministic perceptron neural network", *Neural Networks*, vol. 11, pp. 153–170, 1998.

[TAS 05] TASSOU S.A., GRACE I.N., "Fault diagnosis and refrigerant leak detection in vapour compression refrigeration systems", *International Journal of Refrigeration*, vol. 28, no. 5, pp. 680–688, 2005.

[TSA 05] TSANG I.W., KWOK J.T., LAI K.T., "Core vector regression for very large regression problems", *ICML'05: Proceedings of the 22nd International Conference on Machine Learning*, ACM, New York, NY, pp. 912–919, 2005.

[TSO 07] TSO G.K.F., YAU K.K.W., "Predicting electricity energy consumption: a comparison of regression analysis, decision tree and neural networks", *Energy*, vol. 32, no. 9, pp. 1761–1768, 2007.

[VAP 95] VAPNIK V.N., *The Nature of Statistical Learning Theory*, Springer-Verlag, New York, NY, 1995.

[VAP 98] VAPNIK V.N., *Statistical Learning Theory*, Wiley-Interscience, 1998.

[WAN 99] WANG X., CHEN Z., YANG C. *et al.*, "Gray predicting theory and application of energy consumption of building heat-moisture system", *Building and Environment*, vol. 34, no. 4, pp. 417–420, 1999.

[WAN 04] WANG S., XIAO F., "AHU sensor fault diagnosis using principal component analysis method", *Energy and Buildings*, vol. 36, pp. 147–160, 2004.

[WAN 06] WANG S., XU X., "Simplified building model for transient thermal performance estimation using GA-based parameter identification", *International Journal of Thermal Sciences*, vol. 45, no. 4, pp. 419–432, 2006.

[WES 99] WESTERGREN K.-E., HÖBERG H., NORLEN U., "Monitoring energy consumption in single-family houses", *Energy and Buildings*, vol. 29, no. 3, pp. 247–257, 1999.

[WES 00] WESTON J., MUKHERJEE S., CHAPELLE O. *et al.*, "Feature selection for SVMs", *Advances in Neural Information Processing Systems*, vol. 13, pp. 668–674, 2000.

[WES 04] WESTPHAL F.S., LAMBERTS R., "The use of simplified weather data to estimate thermal loads of non-residential buildings", *Energy and Buildings*, vol. 36, no. 8, pp. 847–854, 2004.

[WHI 96] WHITE J.A., REICHMUTH R., "Simplified method for predicting building energy consumption using average monthly temperatures", *Proceedings of the 31st Intersociety Energy Conversion Engineering Conference*, vol. 3, pp. 1834–1839, 1996.

[WIL 94] WILLIAMS R.J., ZIPSER D., *Gradient-Based Learning Algorithms for Recurrent Networks and Their Computational Complexity*, Erlbaum: Hillsdale, NJ, 1994.

[WON 10] WONG S.L., WAN K. K.W., LAM T.N.T., "Artificial neural networks for energy analysis of office buildings with daylighting", *Applied Energy*, vol. 87, no. 2, pp. 551–557, 2010.

[WRI 97] WRIGHT S.J., *Primal-Dual Interior-Point Methods*, SIAM, 1997.

[WU 11] WU S., SUN J.-G., "Cross-level fault detection and diagnosis of building HVAC systems", *Building and Environment*, vol. 46, no. 8, pp. 1558–1566, 2011.

[XIA 06] XIAO F., WANG S., ZHANG J., "A diagnostic tool for online sensor health monitoring in air-conditioning systems", *Automation in Construction*, vol. 15, no. 4, pp. 489–503, 2006,.

[XIA 09] XIAO F., WANG S., XU X., GE G., "An isolation enhanced PCA method with expert-based multivariate decoupling for sensor FDD in air-conditioning systems", *Applied Thermal Engineering*, vol. 29, pp. 712–722, 2009.

[YAL 05] YALCINTAS M., AKKURT S., "Artificial neural networks applications in building energy predictions and a case study for tropical climates", *International Journal of Energy Research*, vol. 29, no. 10, pp. 891–901, 2005.

[YAL 06] YALCINTAS M., "An energy benchmarking model based on artificial neural network method with a case example for tropical climates", *International Journal of Energy Research*, vol. 30, no. 14, pp. 1158–1174, 2006.

[YAL 07] YALCINTAS M., AYTUN OZTURK U., "An energy benchmarking model based on artificial neural network method utilizing US Commercial Buildings Energy Consumption Survey (CBECS) database", *International Journal of Energy Research*, vol. 31, no. 4, pp. 412–421, 2007.

[YAL 08] YALCINTAS M., "Energy-savings predictions for building-equipment retrofits", *Energy and Buildings*, vol. 40, no. 12, pp. 2111–2120, 2008.

[YAN 05] YANG J., RIVARD H., ZMEUREANU R., "On-line building energy prediction using adaptive artificial neural networks", *Energy and Buildings*, vol. 37, no. 12, pp. 1250–1259, 2005.

[YAN 10] YAN C.-W., YAO J., "Application of ANN for the prediction of building energy consumption at different climate zones with HDD and CDD", *Proceedings of 2nd International Conference on Future Computer and Communication*, vol. 3, pp. 286–289, 2010.

[YAN 11] YANG X.-B., JIN X.-Q., DU Z.-M. *et al.*, "A novel model-based fault detection method for temperature sensor using fractal correlation dimension", *Building and Environment*, vol. 46, no. 4, pp. 970–979, 2011.

[YAO 05] YAO R., STEEMERS K., "A method of formulating energy load profile for domestic buildings in the UK", *Energy and Buildings*, vol. 37, no. 6, pp. 663–671, 2005.

[YIK 01] YIK F.W.H., BURNETT J., PRESCOTT I., "Predicting air-conditioning energy consumption of a group of buildings using different heat rejection methods", *Energy and Buildings*, vol. 33, no. 2, pp. 151–166, 2001.

[YOK 09] YOKOYAMA R., WAKUI T., SATAKE R., "Prediction of energy demands using neural network with model identification by global optimization", *Energy Conversion and Management*, vol. 50, no. 2, pp. 319–327, 2009.

[YOO 03] YOON J., LEE E.J., CLARIDGE D.E., "Calibration procedure for energy performance simulation of a commercial building", *Journal of Solar Energy Engineering*, vol. 125, no. 3, pp. 251–257, 2003.

[ZAN 06] ZANNI L., SERAFINI T., ZANGHIRATI G., "Parallel software for training large scale support vector machines on multiprocessor systems", *Journal of Machine Learning Research*, vol. 7, pp. 1467–1492, 2006.

[ZHA 01] ZHANG L., LIN F., ZHANG B., "Support vector machine learning for image retrieval", *International Conference on Image Processing*, pp. 721–724, 2001.

[ZHA 04] ZHANG T., "Solving large scale linear prediction problems using stochastic gradient descent algorithms", *Proceedings of the Twenty-First International Conference on Machine Learning*, ICML'04, ACM, New York, NY, p. 116, 2004.

[ZHA 09] ZHANG Y. M., , QI W. G., "Interval forecasting for heating load using support vector regression and error correcting Markov chains", *Proceedings of the Eighth International Conference on Machine Learning and Cybernetics*, pp. 1106–1110, 2009.

[ZHA 10] ZHAO H.-X., MAGOULÈS F., "Parallel support vector machines applied to the prediction of multiple buildings energy consumption", *Journal of Algorithms & Computational Technology*, vol. 4, no. 2, pp. 231–249, 2010.

[ZHA 12a] ZHAO H.-X., MAGOULÈS F., "Feature selection for predicting building energy consumption based on statistical learning method", *Journal of Algorithms and Computational Technology*, vol. 6, no. 1, pp. 59–78, 2012.

[ZHA 12b] ZHAO H.-X., MAGOULÈS F., "A review on the prediction of building energy consumption", *Renewable and Sustainable Energy Reviews*, vol. 16, no. 6, pp. 3586–3592, 2012.

[ZHO 08] ZHOU Q., WANG S., XU X. *et al.*, "A grey-box model of next-day building thermal load prediction for energy-efficient control", *International Journal of Energy Research*, vol. 32, no. 15, pp. 1418–1431, 2008.

[ZHU 09] ZHU Z.A., CHEN W.Z., WANG G. *et al.*, "P-packSVM: parallel primal grAdient desCent Kernel SVM", *Proceedings of the 9th IEEE International Conference on Data Mining*, pp. 677–686, 2009.

[ZME 02] ZMEUREANU R., "Prediction of the COP of existing rooftop units using artificial neural networks and minimum number of sensors", *Energy*, vol. 27, no. 9, pp. 889–904, 2002.

Index

Other titles from

in

Computer Engineering

2015

BARBIER Franck, RECOUSSINE Jean-Luc
COBOL Software Modernization: From Principles to Implementation with the BLU AGE® Method

CHEN Ken
Performance Evaluation by Simulation and Analysis with Applications to Computer Networks

CLERC Maurice
Guided Randomness in Optimization (Metaheuristics Set - Volume 1)

DURAND Nicolas, GIANAZZA David, GOTTELAND Jean-Baptiste, ALLIOT Jean-Marc
Metaheuristics for Air Traffic Management (Metaheuristics Set - Volume 2)

MAGOULES Frédéric, ROUX François-Xavier, HOUZEAUX Guillaume
Parallel Scientific Computing

MUNEESAWANG Paisarn, YAMMEN Suchart
Visual Inspection Technology in the Hard Disk Drive Industry

2014

BOULANGER Jean-Louis
Formal Methods Applied to Industrial Complex Systems

BOULANGER Jean-Louis
Formal Methods Applied to Complex Systems: Implementation of the B Method

GARDI Frédéric, BENOIST Thierry, DARLAY Julien, ESTELLON Bertrand, MEGEL Romain
Mathematical Programming Solver based on Local Search

KRICHEN Saoussen, CHAOUACHI Jouhaina
Graph-related Optimization and Decision Support Systems

LARRIEU Nicolas, VARET Antoine
Rapid Prototyping of Software for Avionics Systems: Model-oriented Approaches for Complex Systems Certification

OUSSALAH Mourad Chabane
Software Architecture 1
Software Architecture 2

QUESNEL Flavien
Scheduling of Large-scale Virtualized Infrastructures: Toward Cooperative Management

RIGO Michel
Formal Languages, Automata and Numeration Systems 1: Introduction to Combinatorics on Words
Formal Languages, Automata and Numeration Systems 2: Applications to Recognizability and Decidability

SAINT-DIZIER Patrick
Musical Rhetoric: Foundations and Annotation Schemes

TOUATI Sid, DE DINECHIN Benoit
Advanced Backend Optimization

2013

ANDRÉ Etienne, SOULAT Romain
The Inverse Method: Parametric Verification of Real-time Embedded Systems

BOULANGER Jean-Louis
Safety Management for Software-based Equipment

DELAHAYE Daniel, PUECHMOREL Stéphane
Modeling and Optimization of Air Traffic

FRANCOPOULO Gil
LMF — Lexical Markup Framework

GHÉDIRA Khaled
Constraint Satisfaction Problems

ROCHANGE Christine, UHRIG Sascha, SAINRAT Pascal
Time-Predictable Architectures

WAHBI Mohamed
Algorithms and Ordering Heuristics for Distributed Constraint Satisfaction Problems

ZELM Martin *et al.*
Enterprise Interoperability

2012

ARBOLEDA Hugo, ROYER Jean-Claude
Model-Driven and Software Product Line Engineering

BLANCHET Gérard, DUPOUY Bertrand
Computer Architecture

BOULANGER Jean-Louis
Industrial Use of Formal Methods: Formal Verification

BOULANGER Jean-Louis
Formal Method: Industrial Use from Model to the Code

CALVARY Gaëlle, DELOT Thierry, SEDES Florence, TIGLI Jean-Yves
Computer Science and Ambient Intelligence

MAHOUT Vincent
Assembly Language Programming: ARM Cortex-M3 2.0: Organization, Innovation and Territory

MARLET Renaud
Program Specialization

SOTO Maria, SEVAUX Marc, ROSSI André, LAURENT Johann
Memory Allocation Problems in Embedded Systems: Optimization Methods

2011

BICHOT Charles-Edmond, SIARRY Patrick
Graph Partitioning

BOULANGER Jean-Louis
Static Analysis of Software: The Abstract Interpretation

CAFERRA Ricardo
Logic for Computer Science and Artificial Intelligence

HOMES Bernard
Fundamentals of Software Testing

KORDON Fabrice, HADDAD Serge, PAUTET Laurent, PETRUCCI Laure
Distributed Systems: Design and Algorithms

KORDON Fabrice, HADDAD Serge, PAUTET Laurent, PETRUCCI Laure
Models and Analysis in Distributed Systems

LORCA Xavier
Tree-based Graph Partitioning Constraint

TRUCHET Charlotte, ASSAYAG Gerard
Constraint Programming in Music

VICAT-BLANC PRIMET Pascale *et al.*
Computing Networks: From Cluster to Cloud Computing

2010

AUDIBERT Pierre
Mathematics for Informatics and Computer Science

BABAU Jean-Philippe *et al.*
Model Driven Engineering for Distributed Real-Time Embedded Systems 2009

BOULANGER Jean-Louis
Safety of Computer Architectures

MONMARCHE Nicolas *et al.*
Artificial Ants

PANETTO Hervé, BOUDJLIDA Nacer
Interoperability for Enterprise Software and Applications 2010

PASCHOS Vangelis Th
Combinatorial Optimization – 3-volume series
Concepts of Combinatorial Optimization – Volume 1
Problems and New Approaches – Volume 2
Applications of Combinatorial Optimization – Volume 3

SIGAUD Olivier *et al.*
Markov Decision Processes in Artificial Intelligence

SOLNON Christine
Ant Colony Optimization and Constraint Programming

AUBRUN Christophe, SIMON Daniel, SONG Ye-Qiong *et al.*
Co-design Approaches for Dependable Networked Control Systems

2009

FOURNIER Jean-Claude
Graph Theory and Applications

GUEDON Jeanpierre
The Mojette Transform / Theory and Applications

JARD Claude, ROUX Olivier
Communicating Embedded Systems / Software and Design

LECOUTRE Christophe
Constraint Networks / Targeting Simplicity for Techniques and Algorithms

2008

BANÂTRE Michel, MARRÓN Pedro José, OLLERO Hannibal, WOLITZ Adam
Cooperating Embedded Systems and Wireless Sensor Networks

MERZ Stephan, NAVET Nicolas
Modeling and Verification of Real-time Systems

PASCHOS Vangelis Th
Combinatorial Optimization and Theoretical Computer Science: Interfaces and Perspectives

WALDNER Jean-Baptiste
Nanocomputers and Swarm Intelligence

2007

BENHAMOU Frédéric, JUSSIEN Narendra, O'SULLIVAN Barry
Trends in Constraint Programming

JUSSIEN Narendra
A to Z of Sudoku

2006

BABAU Jean-Philippe *et al.*
From MDD Concepts to Experiments and Illustrations – DRES 2006

HABRIAS Henri, FRAPPIER Marc
Software Specification Methods

MURAT Cecile, PASCHOS Vangelis Th
Probabilistic Combinatorial Optimization on Graphs

PANETTO Hervé, BOUDJLIDA Nacer
Interoperability for Enterprise Software and Applications 2006 / IFAC-IFIP I-ESA'2006

2005

GÉRARD Sébastien *et al.*
Model Driven Engineering for Distributed Real Time Embedded Systems

PANETTO Hervé
Interoperability of Enterprise Software and Applications 2005

Lightning Source UK Ltd.
Milton Keynes UK
UKHW011209130619
344322UK00003B/85/P